Surviving with Financial Application Packages for the Computer

GARY D. BROWN

DONALD SEFTON

A Wiley-Interscience Publication
JOHN WILEY & SONS
New York • Chichester • Brisbane • Toronto • Singapore

This publication is designed to provide accurate and
authoritative information in regard to the subject
matter covered. It is sold with the understanding that
the publisher is not engaged in rendering legal, accounting,
or other professional service. If legal advice or other
expert assistance is required, the services of a competent
professional person should be sought. *From a Declaration
of Principles jointly adopted by a Committee of the
American Bar Association and a Committee of Publishers.*

Library of Congress Cataloging in Publication Data:
Brown, Gary DeWard.
    Surviving with financial application packages for the computer.

    "A Wiley-Interscience publication."
    Includes index.
    1. Corporations—Finance—Data processing. 2. Business
enterprises—Finance—Data processing. 3. Accounting—Data
processing. 4. Business—Data processing.
I. Sefton, Donald, 1952– . II. Title.
HG4012.5.B76 1983   658.1'5'0285425   82-23732
ISBN 0-471-87065-X

Printed in the United States of America

10 9 8 7 6 5 4 3 2 1

To Margaret Brown, who never envisioned computer consoles, yet forced her son to take typing in a small Wyoming School.

To Roy Sefton, who insisted that his son learn his ABCs on a typewriter.

Preface

At a seminar we conducted not long ago, a financial vice president asked if it would be possible for his company to have a new computerized general ledger, personnel/payroll, accounts receivable, and accounts payable system installed by year end. It was then October. While the financial vice president viewed it as a two-month job, we knew it would take at least a year and more likely two.

Even at best, any application package is only a qualified success. At worst, it is a disaster. Despite this, application packages are usually better than any alternative.

We intend this book to dispel some of the myths and naïveté about application packages. The book describes methods that will make the selection of an applications package more successful if not easier. Selection will never be easy. The formula for success, however, is easy: Get a chief financial officer or other senior executive who knows what he or she wants and will push until it is done. Data processing's role in application packages is supporting, not leading.

GARY D. BROWN
DONALD SEFTON

Los Angeles, California
March 1983

Contents

Surviving with Financial Application Packages for the Computer

Chapter 1
Introduction

This is a television commercial. Two clean-cut delivery men in white smocks roll a small computer down a hallway as the camera pans back to catch the heads of people peering out their offices to admire the new computer. The computer comes to rest in a spacious office, one of the delivery men plugs it in, and an efficient secretary swoops up to the console and sits down dextrously fingering the keys. The boss comes in.

"Wonderful!" the boss says. "Our new computer has arrived. We can certainly use it. Now we can see how our new sales program is doing on the West Coast."

"I'll have the answer for you in a second," the efficient secretary says, as 10 nimble fingers fly over the keyboard. A graph flashes on the screen and the printer erupts into life.

"Good, very good," the boss says, tearing off the paper from the printer and studying it. "That new product is making excellent progress out there on the West Coast. I think we can expand it into the Southwest now that we have our computer to help us look after things."

The camera pans back again to catch the room full of smiling faces, the music rises, and the commercial fades out.

The popular view of computers and application packages—but it is not like this—ever!

What is a package? It is a collection of programs designed to provide a general solution to a specific or general problem. When you have finished shaking it, dissecting it, and interjecting your company's policy and procedures into it, it will be a system—your company's system, not quite like any other installation of the same product.

This introductory chapter describes for whom the book is written, what it covers, how it is organized, and how the subject is approached.

AUDIENCE

Financial packages are too important to be left to data processing alone. Certainly, the data processing people will be involved—heavily involved. But it takes much more than just data processing to select and install a financial package system.

With application packages, such as financial systems, the end user must become as involved with the selection and implementation as the data processing people. This book addresses all those who will do the selection and implementation. They include, on the end user side, chief financial officers, treasurers, controllers, accounting managers, payroll managers, personnel managers, general accounting, both internal and external auditors, and financial managers.

The book intends to sophisticate the end user. A successful package implementation requires a sophisticated end user. By sophisticated, we mean that an end user should be able to gently remind a data processing person to avoid condescension, since concepts are understood perfectly as long as the discussion has some passing relationship to the English language.

On the data processing side, the audience is the data processing director, systems and programming managers, systems analysts, project managers, and lead programmers.

Much of the problem in package systems comes from the view each side, data processing and end user, has of the other. To the end user, data processing is a group that seems to take forever to get anything done. To the data processing people, end users are a frustrating source of constant change. These problems will be dealt with at some length. The method will be to look at the problems from both the viewpoint of data processing and of the end user, shifting back and forth. This allows each group to see the problems of the other.

SCOPE

Financial packages are available for all computers, varying in size from hand calculators to room-filling, light-dimming behemoths. The field is too large to cover in one book, and hardware and software are changing so fast for the smaller computers that little specific can be said that would not have to be unsaid in a year.

This book concentrates on large sites using large computers. Here the packages and hardware are generally stable and enduring. Since most large computers are IBM or IBM compatible, most financial packages are designed to run on them. The IBM operating system is the de facto standard for large computers. Hence all of the packages described here run on IBM computers. Non-IBM computers present special problems, and these are described in a later chapter. One chapter is included on buying packages for personal computers because all readers are candidates for these packages.

There are three broad categories of software packages: systems tools (such as a disk storage utility), programming tools (such as a report writer), and application packages. Again the field is too broad to cover in one book and the selection and implementation of applications packages have little in common with systems or programming tools. While most of the book is directed toward application packages in general, five specific areas—general ledger, accounts payable, accounts receivable, personnel/payroll, and fixed assets—are covered in detail. These five package areas are applicable to every corporation and are central to their operation.

ORGANIZATION

The first third of the book presents an overview of application packages. It discusses items common to all types of application packages. The middle third of the book covers general ledger, accounts payable, accounts receivable, personnel/payroll, and fixed assets in detail. These chapters are the most technical. The final third tells how to select and implement packages, and is again appropriate for all application packages.

THE TRADITIONAL APPROACH

Let us look for a second at the traditional method of selecting application packages. It goes roughly as follows:

1. Perform a make versus buy analysis.
2. Identify the packages that will run on the computer system.
3. Contact the salesmen for a presentation on each of the packages.
4. Write a Request for Proposal (RFP).
5. Benchmark the application packages.
6. Perform a weighted average analysis on the package features.

7. Select the package, balancing the price against the weighted average analysis.
8. Implement the package.

This is the last you will see of the traditional approach. It wastes time and does not work. Let us look at the steps again to see why.

1. Perform a make versus buy analysis. This is a waste of time. A company should no more perform a make versus buy analysis for an application package than it should for an automobile. A company can never afford to make if it can buy. No analysis is needed. A company buys unless it must make.
2. Identify the packages that will run on the computer system. This step is done, but not here. It is done after writing the RFP. Instead, a requirements study is done. A company must determine what it needs before it does anything else.
3. Contact the salespersons. Of course, the salespersons are eventually contacted, or a selected few of them, but not here. Dealing with them requires a lot of time, and the time is wasted until an RFP is prepared.
4. Prepare the RFP—yes, after the requirements study. But it must be done with the full knowledge that if questions are phrased so that they can be answered yes or no, all the answers from the vendors will be yes. A good salesperson knows that there is always a way to do anything.
5. Benchmark the packages. Probably impractical and a waste of time. It will take a year to implement the application package to run representative data at an installation. This makes benchmarking difficult. Benchmarking with made-up data only tells how well the package performs on the made-up data. It may tell nothing about how the package will perform in production.
6. Perform a weighted average. This is usually done, not to make a decision, but to impress others with the objectivity of the selection process by quantifying it. In practice, people keep tinkering with the weights until the weighted average yields the decision they know is right from less quantifiable means.
7. Selection. This indeed is done, not as a lightning decision made by quantified methods, but by grinding analysis in which the leading candidate survives. And price? Price is about as relevant in selecting a package as it is in selecting a doctor for

open heart surgery. How well the package meets the needs is far more important than price. And anyway, the price of a package is less than half the cost of replacing a system.

8. Implementation. This one is correctly placed, and it is the toughest part of all.

Before going on to the next chapter, there are two observations made from the experience of many package installations that should be kept in mind. First, everyone is an expert. A lawyer whose firm has installed a small computer becomes an authority. Doctors with small computers to do their billings are experts. A data processing manager who has installed a Sort/Merge utility package cannot imagine that installing an applications package can be much different.

The second observation is that a package implementation rarely goes smoothly. Even people who have been through the pain of installing an applications package and have suffered accordingly believe that their situation was unique, and that the problems would never occur again. In a sense they are right. The same problems never recur, but other problems of equal magnitude always do.

Many of you reading this book have been involved in the selection and implementation of an applications package. Consequently, many of the points made in this book are familiar. Part of the purpose of this book is to convince you that such problems are not unique to you or your installation, but must be taken into consideration in every system you implement.

Chapter 2
The Players—
A Case Study

As in many undertakings, the most difficult part in implementing a package is dealing with the people. Perhaps more than anything else, a successful implementation depends on how well the people involved work together. So, while people problems are in no way unique to implementing a package, they still deserve their fair share of attention. What makes implementing a package especially difficult is the animosity that has built up between the end users and data processing. This chapter examines some potential problems through the use of a case study.

In financial package implementation, there is a fairly standard group of people involved. On the data processing side, they include a data processing manager, a project leader, a systems analyst, and programmers. The user side is represented by a chief financial officer (CFO), an assistant, accountants, clerks, a purchasing agent, and an auditor.

Methods and plans frequently are premised upon a staff of willing, dedicated people who always submerge their egos and self-interest to the betterment of the project. This case study looks at package implementation where this does not occur. Somehow, data processing seems to bring out certain traits in people. These traits are examined using a fictitious company. The company is a worst case for package implementation, more closely resembling "General Hospital" than Management Theory 101A. There will never be any people like the ones described in this case study, but our experience in many package implementations, in many companies, makes us believe that the traits usually are present in someone involved in the package.

The case study consists of a moderate-size company that is in the process of replacing an aging applications system with a package.

DATA PROCESSING

Perhaps the toughest job in any company is that of data processing manager. Because the job is so demanding, it often has a high turnover. And so we meet the first data processing person in the company, the recently hired DP manager. She* was hired with great expectations, and has made a good impression so far. Things were a complete mess when she took over—her predecessor was fired. The new DP manager knows that she has about two years in which to turn things around and prove herself. The first year she can coast on her predecessor's failure, but she must have some successes by the second year if she is to survive.

The new DP manager sees the package implementation as a way of proving herself and of looking good to management. Unfortunately, her experience has been mainly in installing operating system packages rather than application packages, and she does not know how much more difficult an application package is. Nonetheless, she has become involved in the package implementation because she has so much at stake.

The new DP manager can be of immense help to the project because she has such a vested interest in its success. Someone needs to spend some time with her to explain what it takes to implement a financial package. Once she understands the steps involved, she will support the package. She is fairly sharp. It is just that her experience with systems packages, which appear to be similar, is actually very different and clouds her viewpoint.

Reporting to the DP manager is the programming project leader, an old-timer who bears scars from years of long nights in the data center. Like a tough army platoon sergeant, he is a little rough around the edges and nobody sees him as a potential for Mahogany Row. But when the chips are down, everyone depends on him to get the job done, and he knows it. He single-handedly solved the payroll tax problem when the much heralded new hot-shot programmer crumbled at the eleventh hour after weeks on the task. The project leader is self-reliant and wary after years of cleaning up the messes and broken promises of his more glib and polished counterparts.

The project leader's weakness is his suspicion of any programs or systems that he has not personally written, and his long experience gives him good justification. He initially fought the package tooth and

*The demographics in this case study are purely random.

nail because he felt he could do it better himself, but he has the most realistic perception in the entire organization of its impact, if only because of his pessimism. Ultimately, he will be the one who implements the package.

The systems analyst assigned to the package implementation is right out of college with a degree in computer science. She is highly motivated and more than willing to share what she knows. She literally brims with the new technology. She can laud, in accurate detail, the virtues of top down design, HIPO flowcharting, modular programming, and recursive techniques, for hours extempore. She is an evangelist about such subjects. At least once a week she bursts into the DP manager's office with a brochure for a seminar that she must attend.

The systems analyst is also a bright, gifted programmer full of enthusiasm about her work. However, her total dedication to the new technology and her heady academic background blind her to some basic data processing realities. Her solution to any maintenance problem is to rewrite the program or system. Called upon by the DP manager to make minor changes in a system, she returned a few hours later with a look on her face like she had just pulled her hand from the entrails of a great rotting tuna.

"Ugh!" the systems analyst said. "How could anyone have signed off on that bowl of spaghetti masquerading as a program? It's a travesty. I know you just wanted me to change a column heading, but give me three weeks and I'll rewrite the whole thing the way it should have been written in the first place. The users will never know; they'll only notice the column heading change."

The systems analyst is right, of course, but this approach is expensive because of the complexity of business applications and the tremendous investment they represent. Also, new programming techniques periodically come into vogue so that rewriting could go on forever. Her academic background assures her that business applications are both mundane and trivial. They certainly do not compare to the complex data structures and esoteric algorithms she used in homework assignments. To her, a payroll system is simply a matter of multiplying rate times hours.

One of the applications programmers assigned to implementing the package has been in data processing for years. He is a product of the time when a programmer's skill was measured by how obscurely he wrote his programs—every program he writes is a tribute to them. His life is dedicated to the quest for the ultimate puzzle—to solve it or create it. Rubik's Cube was a honeymoon for him.

He is a truly gifted programmer, provided that someone does not have to modify or try to understand one of his programs. Unfortunately, his ideal career match, designing burglarproof tombs for Egyptian Pharaohs, died out 30 centuries ago. He was enraptured when he discovered that writing data of various lengths on the new tape drives actually caused them to sing. The weekend he was supposed to be helping the project leader on the payroll tax problem he spent writing a program to play "Ballad of the Green Beret" on the tape drives.

His peculiar skills and penchant for puzzles are very useful in one application—security. He can locate the weakness in any package security system. He should just not write code.

The other applications programmer was recently hired. She has been in the business for a long time, she has impressive credentials, and she gave a great interview. When the new DP manager hired her, she thought she was getting a potential project leader. And it seemed that way until the day the programmer was called on to fix a problem in the accounts payable system. After two days of waiting for the programmer to solve it, the DP manager dropped by her office.

"Hey, what's happening on accounts payable?" the DP manager asked. "Have you got it fixed yet?"

The programmer, who had been staring out the window, sat up quickly. "Yeah, almost," she said, her voice quivering. "It's almost done. I think the DCB got clobbered. I'll have to add some debugging code." Her voice had been rising, and she began talking faster and faster.

"What?" the DP manager said. "Accounting said that it was a truncation problem in the allocation of overhead."

"No . . . Oh yeah, truncation problem. The truncation must have clobbered the DCB. I've go to look at the channel control words to be sure." By now, she was sweating profusely.

"What do channel control words or a DCB have to do with a truncation problem?" the DP manager asked. "Good grief, the problem should have been solved in 15 minutes."

"Right, I've all but got it solved," the programmer said, her hands now shaking.

Eventually, the DP manager had to call on the project leader to solve the problem, which took him 10 minutes. The programmer can no longer handle pressure. She has all the skill and all the knowledge, but if leaned on for support, she crumbles. She can be helpful early in a package implementation, but later on when the pressure builds, she is dangerous to have around.

The final data processing person is the systems programmer, who prefers the company of his beloved computer to any social contact. He refers to computer users as "abusers" and only grudgingly accepts them as a necessary evil to allow him to have access to a computer. He is rather abrasive with people, but no one speaks to him about it because he might split to another company and boost his salary to over $50,000 a year.

The systems programmer will not get involved in the package implementation of his own volition. However, he should be cultivated. He knows the system and can solve problems. He can make things work. He is one of the few people in the company who is a true expert in his job.

This then is the data processing staff. Let us now turn to the end user staff.

THE END USERS

The chief financial officer built the company on courage, audacity, avarice, and a penchant for quick decisions. She is struggling to cope with the change in her company from an aggressive, enterpreneurial organization to a conservative, professionally managed one.

Accustomed to direct involvement in the details of business operations and quick decisions, she is frustrated by the prospect of committing to the structure and rigidity required for computerization. She is often heard to say "In the old days, we didn't need to go through all those confusing adjustments. I just told an accountant to erase it and write it in correctly."

The CFO believes that the key to success depends on the speed and forcefulness of the decisions one makes. She wants things done now, she wants costs to approach zero, and she does not want to hear about anyone's problems in accomplishing this. She is a "shaker" who gets things done. Consequently, she is the best person to head the new systems project. However, she lacks patience and has little appreciation for what it takes to implement a package.

The CFO must be educated, a difficult task because she does not believe that she can be wrong. Her final argument will always be: "Well, I built this company. When you've built a company from 5 million in sales to 200 million, then you can tell me what decisions to make."

The success of this package implementation is largely dependent on her. If she knows what she wants and pushes to get it done, the package will be a success. If not, it will likely fail.

Reporting to the CFO is her assistant, a B-school graduate from a prestigious Eastern business school. With two programming classes and an operations research seminar under his belt, he is ready to make the world safe from data processing. He is greatly feared in data processing because he embodies the cliché "a little knowledge is dangerous." Also, his reputation and credentials are impeccable and top management views him as being bilingual, speaking both the data processing and business dialects.

The assistant owns a personal computer and, because of his vast experience with it (including writing a program to balance his checkbook and several hundred hours of playing space war games), he feels obligated to sit in judgment upon all that transpires in data processing. His recommended solution to most problems is a microcomputer. Having inventory problems? Get a micro. Running out of disk space on your 3081? Get a micro. Having trouble obtaining time sheets from your oil exploration crew being held hostage by crazed ruffians in the Arabian desert? Send them a micro.

The assistant's real problem is that it is difficult for him to learn because he has made the assumption that he knows everything. His role in the package implementation will be to be constantly amazed that things take so long and do not go smoothly as they did in his textbooks.

The accountant working on the package implementation does not understand computers, but he professes full confidence in data processing. "You just do it the way you know best. I don't know anything about computers myself." When a system is delivered, the accountant is pleased until he finds a problem. Then he gets a doe-eyed, injured innocent look, his lower lip quivers, he sighs deeply, and sinks back into his chair in complete dejection.

The accountant's problem is that he sees either perfection or disaster, with no middle ground. After a week on the job, the DP manager received the following telephone call from the accountant:

"Your system doesn't work," the accountant said, not bothering to say hello.

"What do you mean?" the DP manager said. She knew it was the accountant because he calls her about twice a day.

"It's all wrong," the accountant said.

"What's all wrong?" the DP manager responded.

"Your system, that's what. It's all wrong. I just thought you'd like to know." To the accountant, it is always "your" system when something goes wrong.

"Yes, but what? What's all wrong?"

"Everything. It doesn't work."

After sparring like this for a while, the DP manager went down to the accountant's office and discovered that a payroll clerk had entered the wrong number of deductions for a new hire, and the employee complained. The accountant considers this ample evidence that the payroll system is totally unusable.

The way to work with this accountant is to get him to commit himself on paper. Maneuver him to where he is made to put down on paper what he needs, and to acknowledge that future requirements coming out of left field will be his fault and not the project's. It also helps to establish a set of ground rules with him to cover such things as accounting's responsibility to look at error reports.

The accounting clerk picked to help with the package implementation has been with the company since before World War II, and is on a first-name basis with all the past chairmen of the board. She knows more about the firm's accounting than anyone, but she never really made the transition from a manual accounting environment to the computer. She is the only one in the company with a crank adding machine. She distrusts the computer. She feels that if something cannot be done by hand, there is something immoral about it.

The clerk became somewhat comfortable in a batch computer environment but is totally overwhelmed by a terminal in an on-line environment. She thinks of it as a weird TV set containing great piles of wire that will break if she uses it.

The clerk has invaluable information about the existing system, manual or computer, but she does not realize it. It is difficult for her to abstract. She has used the system for 10 years and knows all of its vagaries and problems. However, when pressed, she will plead ignorance and say "Gee, I just fill out these forms and get these reports back."

The clerk is submissive, trusting, and accepts decisions, policies, and procedures much like the weather—"Gosh, it's terrible, but what can anyone do about it?" Sadly, the clerk is likely to be the first casualty in the installation of the new system. Either someone above will determine beforehand that she will not be able to adapt to change or she will quit because of the frustration during conversion.

The clerk can be invaluable in the selection and implementation of a package system if her participation and not just her compliance can be elicited. She must be made to realize that the new system will be different and that her job will be different. Otherwise, the system will just frighten her. Any new work or data that she must provide will be questioned with: "Well, if it's a new system, why do I have more work instead of less? Isn't that why we're replacing the old system?" By the same token, any work eliminated is viewed as threatening: "I always did that on Tuesdays and Thursdays. What will I do now? Will I lose my job?"

Outside of the accounting department, we encounter the crusty purchasing agent. He can make a deal to purchase anything from a refrigerator to dehydrated yak steak. He is a retired Navy man who earned his reputation by keeping the entire Seventh Fleet supplied with black-market Haagen-Dazs ice cream during its sixth-month cruise of the Indian Ocean.

The purchasing agent is accustomed to being the final authority on any purchase. In fact, he does a fantastic job on buying envelopes, desk calculators, typewriters, company cars, and even computers. Unfortunately, his mind set makes it difficult to convince him that someone really must have a specific product and not something that appears similar to it. Just last year, he was asked to order number 10 envelopes from a specific vendor and he found identical stationery for a third the price from one of his vendors. He sees no reason why application packages should not be bought the same way. He will be hard to convince otherwise.

The goal with the purchasing agent should be to get him out of the picture entirely. He does not belong in package selection.

The company's internal auditor, because he specializes in EDP audit, will become involved in the package implementation. He relishes his role of reviewing the propriety of the actions of others. He does not want to make rules; he wants to apply them. To him, rules are an end in themselves. His job as auditor gives him full rein to exercise his love of rules and his basic suspicion about the deviousness of people.

The auditor makes the rounds every year or so to verify that the accounting and data processing systems are being properly maintained, used, and documented. He always finds something wrong— he must: that is his job. He is not so much interested in how things actually work as he is in the written procedures. Quality of documentation to the auditor is more a matter of heft and feel than of reasonableness. Nothing is real to him without documentation. If the paperwork were all in order, he probably would not notice that the computer operators had backed up a semi truck to the computer room and were busily shoveling Apple computers into the truck.

The auditor is particularly good at finding inconsistencies in the documentation and controls. Unfortunately, it is difficult to get him to identify holes while the system is being designed. He prefers to lie in wait until the system is placed in production.

The auditor is actually a valuable asset, irritating though he may be. He serves as a constant reminder that systems are vulnerable and security inadequate. He can make an invaluable contribution on the front end of system development if he can be made to participate and share his penchant for finding faults. This is difficult for him because he trusts hindsight far more than foresight. He finds it difficult to participate in decisions. His comfortable role is to find faults later.

These then are the players in our case study. In implementing a package, a few of these traits—and perhaps others—may have to be dealt with. People all have their own idiosyncrasies. The chapters that follow discuss various problems as they affect the players.

Knowing the players is just part of the problem. Another part is the relationship between the end users and data processing. Early in the writing of this book, the authors mused together that end users are always unhappy with data processing. In only one instance of our collective experience could we think of an organization where data processing was held in any esteem. We could think of none in which data processing held the end users in esteem. This experience spans employment and consulting in industries as diverse as public utilities, banks, aerospace, research, hospital and medical, the oil industry, and a host of manufacturers. It appears all but universal.

The following section continues the case study by examining how the end users see data processing and how data processing views the end users. Since the case study represents a worst case, the views of each side are unfair and inaccurate, but perhaps they have a core of truth.

VIEW OF THE END USER

If we were to walk through our fictitious company and talk to end users about data processing, the following remarks would be typical.

"What do I think about data processing? I don't think much about it at all. The computer is incidental to my work. It's one of the tools that my department uses to accomplish our primary task. If the computer can help us, fine. Otherwise, we would rather live without it."

"You shouldn't ask me about data processing. I don't trust it. To me, data processing is a department that promises it can do everything, takes incredibly long to do anything, and is inordinately expensive. Data processing is staffed by a strange collection of overpaid people who tend to be prima donnas. They often become so engrossed with the computer that they lose sight of what the computer is intended to do. They seem happiest when curled up to a warm terminal, reading a memory dump. As far as I'm concerned, data processing people are a bunch of flakes who spend a lot of money and don't generate any revenue."

□□□

"Data processing, huh? The thing that amazes me is that I keep reading that computer hardware yields a tenfold increase in price/performance every decade. What I want to know is why my computing bill somehow keeps increasing, why the computer is always overloaded, and why an individual job seems to cost as much as always to run on the computer. I can't keep up with the new systems that data processing keeps adding. Every year we seem to go from VS to MVS to TSO to CMS to IMS to CICS to SPF to whatever. They get piled in layers on the computer. The result seems to be that the computer system is often down. Even when the computer is up, it seems that when I hit the ENTER key from a terminal, nothing happens for several minutes."

□□□

"I'll tell you what's wrong with data processing people. They're obsessed with efficiency. I have to go through all kinds of contortions if I want to use their systems. I wanted to store some data on the computer once, and they told me I had to learn an entire job control language. I was supposed to tell the computer what block size and how many tracks to allocate. How do I know these things? The computer ought to be able to figure things like this out for itself.

When I use the computer, I'm concerned with function, not efficiency. I know what I want done, and I'm not interested in what the computer can do or how it does it. All data processing seems interested in is what the computer can do and how it does it."

□□□

"What I don't like about data processing are systems programmers. They remind me of Egyptian priests under the Pharaohs. They know all the magic rites to make the Nile flood each year, and they expect due homage from mere mortals. They seem to have a total disdain for anyone who wants to put the computer to productive work. They also have an uncanny knack for developing jargon and acronyms that shield us from the fact that much of what they do can actually be understood. Every so often, these priests step back from one of their creations, term it 'user friendly'—if that happens to be the phrase at the time—and congratulate themselves on a job well done."

□□□

"My department doesn't get along with data processing very well. If you ask me, I think our relationship with data processing is going to worsen. Data processing people, clearly not an inherently social breed, will not change. But now several of us in my department are learning something about data processing. We will no longer pay homage to the data processing priesthood. Already, we're using tools developed for us to produce reports in hours that it took programmers weeks to produce. Data processing seems to believe that it is immoral to write in anything but COBOL.

"My department knows a lot about computing, and although it is mainly on personal computers, large computers can't be that much different."

☐☐☐

"I don't understand why data processing people feel they have to get involved in our selecting a financial package. We're not novices. We have professional experience with acquiring. We've acquired office equipment, parts, office space, and even other companies. We've set up entire purchasing departments to do acquiring. Purchasing a software package is no problem. We just turn over the RFP for software to our purchasing department."

☐☐☐

"There's one question about data processing I've always wanted to ask. Why does it take so long to develop and implement software? Software can't be as difficult as building a bridge or a building. Why should installing a package take longer than building them?

"Why are computer systems so difficult to change? The computer people keep telling us how flexible their systems are, but then when we request a change it takes three years to do it. I'm clear on one thing: computers are inherently inflexible, not flexible. All that talk about flexibility is a lot of nonsense."

☐☐☐

"I don't know if it's data processing people who are the problem so much as computers. The abstractness of computer software makes it difficult for me to evaluate it. I want to evaluate software, and the vendor's salespeople show me glossy brochures. I never get to see the product itself. It's not like buying a used car where I can kick the tires while the salesperson is telling me what a cream puff it is. There is nothing to counterbalance the vendor's sales materials except a lot of work in evaluation.

"When I'm selecting an applications package, all I hear is what the package can do. I get overwhelmed with its capabilities. Then when the package is implemented, all I hear is what it can't do. I feel like the King of Spain, suffering from the 'Spanish Armada Syndrome': You know, the King of Spain looks out at the thousand ships at anchor in the harbor, while all his admirals tell him that England is a pushover. Two months later, a few derelict ships limp back into the harbor. Evidently, ships anchored in a harbor are different from ships in a stormy channel facing an English fleet."

THE VIEW OF DATA PROCESSING

Having let the end users savage data processing, let us now reverse the roles. Imagine ourselves in the same company asking data processing people what they think about the end users.

"What do I think about end users? They're a pain. They scream at my costs, my estimates, and my product. Yet they won't share the responsibility for them. The users are a part of the problem, but they don't want to be a part of the solution. I'm forced to provide not just tools, but solutions to problems. The users' fear of computers forces me to be aggressive, with the result that the users think I'm being self-serving."

□□□

"The thing that gripes me about end users is that they are always complaining about costs. Data processing budgets and costs keep growing and are constantly being compared to the company's growth. The users aways bring up the fact that our costs have gone up tenfold when sales have only tripled. Well, there's a good reason. Information requirements have not tripled or even gone up tenfold; they have gone up twentyfold. In 1970, the company had a few batch systems. Today, we have an on-line network serving all of the corporate locations, and data processing is providing output to the government, the unions, the stockholders, the accountants, the managers, and even individual employees and their spouses."

□□□

"What bugs me about end users is that they always complain about how long things take. If I'm late with a project, it's because I'm not allowed to progress as scheduled. Requirements change. There's always the last minute 'Oh yeah, and it has to accept quarterly budgets.

That's not a big change, is it?' My projects turn out like a person walking up a down escalator: two steps forward and one step back. Why can't the end users accept responsibility for the impact of a change during development. They would never think of telling a contractor to add a bedroom in the middle of construction of a new house, but they'll ask me for a budgeting feature in the middle of implementing a general ledger system. Every project must be finished immediately, without cost, and with the flexibility to anticipate any whim or idiosyncrasy that might eventuate.

"End users blind themselves to some simple realities. Take the usual case of implementing a new system. The end users may want it done by year end. I may say that it'll take 10 months, but since it is now January, the schedule can be met. But then for a variety of reasons the project does not begin until June. The end users see me still committed to a year-end implementation, remembering the 'It can be implemented by year end,' and not 'It will take 10 months.' The time can't be made up, although I'll try. After all, there are 24 hours in a day and seven days in a week. But there is really no way I can make it up. Nothing can change the fact that the equation for an implementation date is: implementation date equals start date plus elapsed time."

☐☐☐

"What bothers me about end users is that they don't realize what it's like to work with a computer that requires us to be absolutely precise, analyzes every step we take, and slaps our hands if we do something wrong. End users don't understand the pressure in data processing. They have never had to solve a complex payroll problem in two hours in order for there to be a payday. Last week I had to make exactly the right changes to exactly the right lines in a 120,000-line program and hope that I didn't introduce an unexpected side effect. This requires great concentration, but to the end users, it was only evidence that I was antisocial."

☐☐☐

"I get tired of the end users always talking about us programmers job hopping. I realize that we tend to have a short tenure, but little effort is made to improve our situation and make us a part of the organization. We have no opportunity to enter into upper management or even make lateral moves into other areas in the corporation. Our promotion must come from within data processing. That's why we change jobs so frequently."

☐☐☐

"I sometimes feel that my whole relationship with end users is like a Catch 22. I'm expected to know and understand everything that the users do, even though they themselves often don't understand it. On the other hand, the users either know nothing of what I do or profess to know my job better that I because they used a home computer to play Pac-Man.

☐☐☐

"I think it's wrong to let end users do their own programming. I had a customer who came to me with a program he had written in a few hours using one of these 'user friendly' end user languages. It was costing $2000 a month to run. I rewrote it in COBOL and reduced the run cost to $500 a month. It only took me a couple of months to write it. It points out the danger of letting end users do their own programming.

"I had another customer who wanted a report almost immediately. I didn't have time to write it in COBOL, so I used a report writer. All I got were complaints. 'I want to print the full page title on only the first page. I want to indent the rows. I want to print some totals in the page heading.' It went on and on and on. The person wanted the report immediately, but then he wanted all the goodies in the report too.

"End users don't recognize the need to compromise what is ideal with what is possible. Any applications system represents a series of compromises. All computer systems have limitations, and these limitations mean that end users will have to make accommodations. Computers are often touted as tools that can do anything, and they can't. End users must accept the fact that there will be compromises and accommodations required of them."

☐☐☐

"We're going to be selecting a financial package soon. I don't look forward to it. I'll probably bear the entire responsibility for identifying needs and selecting the proper package. I'll certainly bear all the blame when it doesn't do everything the users want, including those things they forgot to tell me about.

"I'll be expected to install the package in the time it takes to plug in a radio, despite there being at least a year's worth of work to do. The end users will assume I know everything about the package, all 120,000 lines of it, not one of which I wrote. They'll probably feel that I have diminished mental capacity if I can't answer all questions instantly.

"The package salesman will take the users to football games while I'm busy nights and weekends trying to make the package perform as promised. When it doesn't, the vendor's people will play upon the end users' darkest suspicions about me. It will not be a limitation in their package, but rather my ability that is at fault.

"What bothers me most about installing a package is that I was hired to create new systems. Now I'll be relegated to the role of care-taker for a package already written. I'll work nights and weekends for months to get the package into production only to discover that the end users believe that the package should have been installed and been printing checks in four hours. Oh well, maybe it's better in some other company."

The point of this case study is that the truly difficult problems in implementing an applications package are not technical. The prob-lems of coordinating and dealing with people are far more difficult.

Chapter 3
Impact of Changing
a System

If a company is considering installing a financial system, it will likely be replacing another computerized system. That is, it will be going to a new generation of computer system as opposed to converting a manual system to a computer system. No matter how well the conversion is done and how smoothly the conversion goes, it will be difficult. This chapter examines why. We look first at what it takes to implement a system, what life is like while it is being implemented, and then go over in some detail why it takes so long.

WHAT IT TAKES TO IMPLEMENT A SYSTEM

A package system, from the time the selection is begun until it is implemented, will take well over a year. During this time, someone must perform a requirements study to determine the needs, write a Request for Proposal (RFP) to communicate the needs to the vendors, sit through vendor presentations and go over the RFP with them, and probably visit other installations that have installed the package. Then someone must make the selection, negotiate the contract, and begin the real job, which is the implementation. It is almost impossible to prevent a year from sliding by during just the implementation.

Since installing an applications package is difficult and time-consuming, a company should install a package only if it wants it and wants it badly. Replacing a financial system is not like buying a new car where it takes 10 minutes to become accustomed to the latest model. Financial systems are not replaced just because they are getting old and have many miles on them.

A better analogy in replacing a system is that of a shipwrecked sailor clinging to a log. Off in the distance he sees a tropical island paradise. He would certainly rather be on the island than clinging to his log, but if he lets go and starts swimming, he may drown on the way or be eaten by sharks. Clinging to a log beats this. While people will not drown or be eaten by sharks in installing a new system, the perils are nonetheless there.

LIFE DURING A CHANGE

Because package systems require more user involvement, they place more of a burden on the end users than would an internal system. Installing a new system is more than just hard work, especially for the end users, who have double work. People in accounting must continue all their normal duties, and, in addition, spend the time necessary to learn and implement the new system. In this respect, data processing people are more fortunate than the end users. Installing new systems may be the main job of the data processing department, whereas installing a new system is an addition to the duties of accounting or personnel people. It is for this reason that much of the actual effort in installing the system finally is picked up by data processing.

Implementing a new system and converting from an old one causes a great deal of turmoil. Questions are raised, answered, forgotten, and asked again. People work hard, become worried about how things are going, spend a lot of time writing explanatory memos, develop a concern about the way the new system will affect their jobs, and permit their tempers to become frayed. In trying to keep the old system running while learning and converting to the new system, people become confused and make mistakes. During the last phase of the conversion, everyone involved will be in a constant state of anger.

A new system can have a rippling effect when it plunks down in the middle of an organization. People one would never expect will feel the waves and come forward with their ideas and complaints. Auditors, line managers, the legal staff, government agencies, and even customers can be affected. A new system may be the result of a change in the style of doing business; in fact, it may be the agent of change to force a new style of doing business.

Needless to say, when a lot of people are affected by a change, not all of them will be happy about the changes being made. Even the purchasing agent will have an opinion of what should really be done. (He has located a war surplus system.) There is nothing like the installation of a new system to bring out the organic expertise in everyone, from the janitorial staff to the board of directors. Financial systems are like politics—everyone is an expert and everyone has an opinion.

As the currents of change sweep through an organization, many toes get stepped on, and some vested interests suffer. Everyone becomes upset and confused; some quit the company. People are tired, In short, it is business as usual.

WHY IT TAKES SO LONG TO INSTALL A FINANCIAL PACKAGE

It will take about a year to install a financial system after it is selected, and it will cost about as much to install it as the purchase price of the package.

There are two reactions one might have to this statement. The well-worn programming manager, would say: "A year? At least!" The CFO, would say: "A year? You're crazy. How can it possibly take that long. I don't believe it. Besides, I need it by January so it will take only three months."

It is a little difficult to explain just why it will take a year. Certainly it would not take so long if all went well and nothing unexpected happened. Equally certain is that much will go wrong and the unexpected will happen. Perhaps an analogy can explain this better.

Suppose we were in a strange city, perhaps Los Angeles, which certainly qualifies as a strange city, and we were given a new Ferrari in which to commute to work. The trip is 40 miles, and we quickly compute how long it will take: 40 miles at 150 miles per hour plus 5 minutes for acceleration and braking would mean the trip should take roughly 21 minutes. Simple arithmetic.

But when we start out, we find we can't go 150 miles per hour on the city streets, we miss a few stop lights, we get tied up in traffic, and we even get lost on the way. In a Ferrari, we will probably need to refuel, and there is some chance we will break down. The trip could take two hours.

Of course, that would only happen to someone else, not to us. Others might run out of gas, get lost, or take surface streets when they could get there by freeway, but we would not make those mistakes. It is easy to see the mistakes of others after they have made them and to believe that we could avoid them. But what we fail to realize is that most of the mistakes were unforeseeable. Could one foresee which traffic lights would be missed? Could one foresee where they would get lost? Could one foresee how long they would be slowed by traffic? Could one foresee a breakdown? It is the same in installing a financial package.

If we were to make the same trip in our car each day, and each day the trip were to take two hours, we would finally become convinced that it was a two-hour trip. It is this same reason that leads us to say that implementing a financial package will take about a year.

There is another reason people cannot believe that it will take a year to install a financial system: "It can't take a year because we need it sooner." When people need something immediately they sometimes consider the physical laws that govern speed to be irrelevant. They become like Queen Victoria on a boat trip back from Ireland during a storm. "My compliments to the captain," she said, "but could he arrange to not have the boat rock so?" If the physical laws do not bend for an empress, they are even less likely to do so for a corporate officer.

Even if one believes that it will take a long time to install a financial package, often it is difficult to hold to their estimate when everyone else seems to think it should not take that long. There will probably come a time when someone is making a presentation on the schedule to install a financial package and a vice president will lean back, take a couple of puffs on his pipe, and say that he has just installed the VisiCalc package on his Apple computer. "It took me just a few minutes to install it, and within an hour, I was using it for budgeting. Now you're telling me that it is going to take a year to install a financial package? Shucks, I've installed packages in 15 minutes."

Even experienced data processing managers fall prey to this fallacy. Perhaps they have installed a Sort/Merge package. It would probably take half an hour, and thereafter, everyone at the installation would be using the new Sort/Merge package without even being aware of it. This type of experience has no relevance to financial packages.

Packages like VisiCalc and Sort/Merge are tools. They do not retain data, they simply perform a well-defined, discrete task. The difference between installing them and a financial package is the difference between selecting a new hammer and building a prefabricated house. A hammer is a tool that performs a well-defined task. It is easy to use such tools. But a house, even prefabricated, is a large undertaking. Just securing the building permits and zoning variances can become a career.

Ultimately, it will take a year to install a financial package because there is a year's worth of work to do. And it cannot be speeded up by adding more staff. Adding more people sometimes results in longer implementation times because the people must coordinate their efforts. As Frederick Brooks pointed out in *The Mythical Man-Month*, adding people to a project can make it take longer.[1]

The last third of this book contains a detailed description of the steps required to implement an applications package. It will be apparent from reading these chapters that there is indeed a year's work.

SUMMARY

Installing a package is a large undertaking. As a rule of thumb, it will take a year. During that time, there will be turmoil, hard work—even double work for some—and there will be change. The package installation will take a year primarily because there is a year's worth of work that must proceed sequentially, making it difficult to collapse the time schedule by adding people. It also takes longer than expected because things go wrong and because the unexpected occurs.

REFERENCE

1. Frederick P. Brooks, Jr., *The Mythical Man-Month*, Addison-Wesley, Reading, MA, 1975.

Chapter 4
Why Not a Package?

Computer software is a unique product. It is a product in which all the "manufactured" units are identical. Unlike automobiles, for example, there are no individual lemons. All the products are exactly alike until the manufacturer changes models. It would seem the ideal thing to purchase, and often, but not always, it is. This chapter examines some of the advantages and disadvantages of buying an applications package.

The obvious advantages are cost, time, and staffing. The less obvious ones are the more general design, the fact that the package is a known quantity, that the documentation is better, that training is provided, that maintenance and enhancements can be bought, and that there is a community of users of the package. The main disadvantage of a package is that it may not be suited to the job that needs to be done.

DEVELOPMENT COST, TIME, AND STAFFING

The cost of a package is much lower than that of an internally developed system. To see the difference, let us examine a moderate size package consisting of about 50,000 COBOL source statements. The package would require the following to develop internally:[1,2,3,4]

Average cost/source statement to develop = \$12
\$12 × (50,000 source statements) = \$600,000
Suppose we assign four programmers to the project
Average programmer productivity to develop = 15 statements/day
50,000 statements/(15 statements/day)/(4 programmers) = 3.4 years

These figures are industry averages, and they include the time to design, test, and document. The numbers are very poor predictors of what will be estimated on a computer project. A 50,000-statement system would probably be estimated to cost \$200,000 and take a year. However, the numbers are very good predictors of what it would actually take to implement the system. Computer systems often require three times what is estimated.

By contrast, 50,000 lines of COBOL source statements in an applications package would cost somewhere between $25,000 and $100,000 to purchase, and an equal amount to implement.

This wide discrepancy in numbers eliminates one step in the selection process: the make versus buy decision. There is often as little need for a make versus buy decision in software applications as there is in buying a car. No sane person would perform a make versus buy decision in acquiring a car because of the economic and time constraints. Likewise with application systems. The make versus buy decision for applications comes at the very end, and then it is not really a decision at all. If a company cannot buy what it needs, it is forced to make it. There is little analysis required.

OTHER BENEFITS OF A PACKAGE

When an applications package is bought, there is more to it than just the software. There are several other things that have both an immediate and a long term benefit. Let us see what they are.

The Design

The design is bought. It is a design that was done by experienced people who know the applications area well, and who have the needs of a community of users in mind. Software houses, because they specialize in software, are able to attract highly qualified people. Because the software that they produce is their business, software houses take their designs very seriously.

An internally developed system is designed to meet the current needs of a specific company. The system will try to anticipate future needs too, but most future needs are impossible to anticipate. By contrast, a package system is developed for a wide client base and provides more than is needed by any one company. It represents a consortium of needs across a wide range of companies. Thus while a company may not initially need a feature, if it later needs the feature, it may already be there to use.

Because packages are more generalized than internally developed systems, they can often respond more quickly to change. They are usually table driven, which makes change easy. They come supplied with report writers, which makes adding new reports easy. They provide space in the master file records for adding new fields. They provide user exists at key points to permit a clean interface to do something not provided in the package. None of these features would likely be designed into an internally developed system.

The Unknown

An internally developed system must be accepted on faith until it is implemented. Before implementation, there is only some design documentation and the trust one has in the systems analysts and programmers. With the 18-month average tenure in programming, the system will probably not be completed by those who started it, and so the systems analysts and programmers are also unknown quantities. It is difficult not to have a queasy feeling in one's stomach when starting a large, internally developed applications system.

By contrast, the applications package is a known quantity. It exists and is running in production at other companies. A person can call those companies and talk to the people who implemented it and those who are using it. They can visit them, run their fingers through the output, and heft the manuals with their hands. They can talk to the users and watch the lights blink on the computer when it runs.

The Documentation

The documentation is bought. Software houses have a wide audience for their software and they put a great deal of effort into the documentation. Their documentation represents the only tangible part of their product. It is the first thing customers can see and touch. The internal auditor can ruffle through it and count the pages. The documentation for an applications package is invariably more complete and of a higher quality than internal documentation. It is also kept up to date. Even the best internally developed documentation is likely to become obsolete quickly.

An internally developed system usually suffers from lack of documentation. The programmers who developed the system are within the company, and the unstated feeling is that their presence obviates the need for extensive documentation. Besides, they are too busy to document, and the project is probably way over budget. But soon the 18-month average tenure of a programmer within a company catches up, and the system must live on without its developers in the company.

The Training

The training is bought. The software house has people who are hired to train, and have learned the software in order to teach others how to use it. They have available a staff of experts, they often provide a hot line to answer questions, and they have a breadth of experience to draw upon. They may have prepared many educational materials.

The training is usually conducted by people who are capable of training. In an internally developed system, this responsibility usually is given to data processing people who are notoriously bad at training. Imagine a systems programmer, being dragged out into the daylight to train accounting clerks on how to use a terminal. "The first thing you've got to understand," the systems programmer will say, "is that this is a full duplex system that runs at 9600 baud with mark parity." One end user compared data processing's approach to training end users like trying to get a drink from a fire hose. "You want a drink? Here, take this." Blast!

The Maintenance and Enhancements

Maintenance and enhancements are bought. These two items are perhaps the most significant advantages of package systems. Maintenance is the dominant activity in data processing departments today, with 40 to 60% of the programmer effort going into maintaining current systems.[5] With package systems, the maintenance can be purchased. This includes correction of bugs as well as changes and enhancements. While the maintenance cost will not go to zero for a package, it will be much less than for an internally developed system.

Bug correction is important, but of lesser importance than changes and enhancements. Package systems, because of their wide customer base, extensive use in different circumstances, and quality control of the vendor, usually are more error-free than internally developed systems. There will still be errors, but there should be fewer. Also, the vendor is responsible for correcting bugs.

Vendors offer enhancements that keep their systems alive in the marketplace and adapting to new environments. If a company begins to feel an overwhelming urge to have on-line data entry and validation, it is likely that the package vendor is thinking along these same lines. Package vendors respond to the needs of their customers for enhancements, and this not only provides new capabilities, but can extend the life of the package as well.

Of the 40 to 60% of data processing effort that goes into maintenance, about 70% is for changes and enhancements.[5] This means that
changes and enhancements are the important maintenance items. For
example, a good vendor of a payroll package will send out corrections
as necessary for changes in state tax, federal tax, FUI, FICA, and all
the other regulated deductions. A fixed asset vendor must respond to
any tax rule changes for depreciation. A good personnel/payroll system will be kept current with EEO, OSHA, and ERISA requirements.
These changes are constant, often illogical, and as impossible to anticipate as a Hollywood marriage.

The Community of Users

The fact that an applications package is designed to suit the needs of a
community of users rather than a single user is an important advantage, assuming it is the right community of users. An applications
package provides features that an individual design might not consider. An internally developed payroll package, for example, might
handle payroll taxes for a single state. A payroll package must handle
taxes for all 50 states, and if the Virginias or Carolinas unite into a
single state, or if the Virgin Islands are admitted as a state, the payroll
packages will undoubtably handle them too. Many of the unanticipat-
ed needs that might be devastating to an internally developed package may well be an inherent part of an applications package.

Frequently a package that is developed for a community of users
lessens the impact of change. If the tax laws change, a package vendor
must make the changes, whereas it might require a year for a company
to modify an internally developed system.

For example, a few years ago, the government instituted a request
that companies report FICA on a quarterly rather than annual basis.
This was a big task, even for the package vendors to accomplish, but
with their large customer base, they had to do it. It was a problem for
the package vendors, but not for its customers. For the internally developed payroll system, it was in many cases a disaster. In fact, it was
so difficult for them that the government finally relented and with-
drew the request. Often the government is less benign—and who
knows, perhaps they will reinstitute the change in the future.

Because there are many customers using an application package,
there are many people who are experts on it. Questions can be ad-
dressed not only to the vendor, but also to other users. If the experts
on the system within a company terminate, there is at least some
chance an outsider can be hired who already knows a vendor's system,

but no outsider knows an internally developed system. If an accounting expert on a fixed assets system is promoted, it may be possible to hire another accountant who has worked with the system before.

The community of users often has an organization that can exert influence on the vendor. With annual maintenance about 10% of a package's purchase price, if a package costing $50,000 has a customer base of 500 users, there is a potential annual income of $2,500,000 from maintenance. An amount of $2,500,000 can swing a lot of weight with a vendor.

DISADVANTAGES OF A PACKAGE

If there were only advantages to packages, all applications would be done using them. There are, however, some disadvantages.

A package will be less well known within a company, at least for a while, than an internally developed system. Because both data processing and the end users are involved in the design of an internal system, they end up knowing it inside and out. Generally, both data processing and end users end up knowing applications packages outside, but not inside. They have little reason or incentive to get into the internals of the package and will not know it as well.

This affects the programming staff more than the users. The users have extensive documentation to fall back on, and if that fails, they can call the vendor, who maintains a support staff to answer questions. The lack of knowledge about the internals of a package affects the programming staff if modifications must be made to it, and so modifications should be avoided or held to a minimum.

This disadvantage is not serious. An applications package does not need to be known inside and out to be used. Sometimes it is more difficult to answer questions for an applications package than for an internally developed system, assuming that the developers of the internal system are still with the company, but that is the only effect. And even this has a benefit. Often, programmers continually tinker with an internally developed system to make it more efficient, or whatever, with the usual unhappy results.

Figure 1 is the learning curve of internally developed systems and applications packages. Notice that initially the internally developed system is known better, but later in the system's life when the developers have moved on to other projects or have left the company, an applications package pulls ahead because of its better documentation.

More often, the limited knowledge of the internals of a package

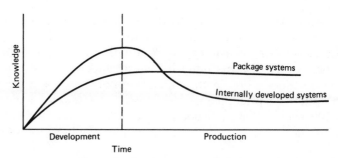

Figure 1.   Learning curves for systems.

affects what is a major portion of maintenance—answering questions. Much of the maintenance effort in a system comes from answering questions. The "Can we do this?" "What happens if we do that?" "Why did it do this?" type of thing. Because the maintenance programmer is less familiar with the system, it will be more difficult to answer such questions, thus in this respect, at least, the maintenance is more difficult.

A more serious disadvantage to a package is that it may not meet special needs. All companies have special needs, and they will have special needs that a package cannot meet. If the needs are special enough, an applications package may not be suitable. Frequently, however, compromise is required. In areas where vendors know that there will be special needs, they will provide some means for the individual company to insert programming to do what it wants. For example, no payroll package can hope to cover all the benefit programs provided by companies; therefore, an area within the payroll program is reserved for the users to insert their own code, or there will be some user exit, such as a subroutine call to an installation-written subroutine that contains whatever special programming is needed.

One mistake frequently made by those acquiring packages is the assumption that just because an applications package is being used by 500 or 1000 companies, it must provide everything needed by their company. This is never so. It is simply amazing how many unique needs every company has. It is different with an internally developed system, which can provide everything that a company needs, or at least everything someone thinks a company needs.

The main problem of package selection is to identify these special needs and to find out if a package can somehow handle them. Not meeting the special needs is perhaps the only legitimate reason for not selecting a package.

A subtle disadvantage of an applications package is that it requires more involvement of the end users, especially at the start when the requirements study is done, when the RFP is written, and when the package is selected. This becomes a disadvantage because the end users may not be ready to assume their share of the burden and the responsibility: "Sure we need a new system, but that's data processing's job. I don't have time to worry about that."

It is as much the end user's responsibility to select a package as it is data processing's. With an internally developed system where data processing does the design, programming, testing, and documentation, they have a far greater responsibility. They are always out in front leading the charge. But it is the end users who must lead the charge when an applications package is selected. Their unwillingness to recognize that the cloud of dust behind them signifies that they are leading a charge usually means that an applications package will be a costly failure.

There is one final disadvantage to an applications package that must be mentioned. About half the cost is up front. When a company buys a package, it will spend anywhere from $25,000 to $100,000 before implementation begins. If the project is canceled two days later, the company will not get any of this money back. The cost of an internally developed system is incremental. In the long run, it may cost five times as much as installing a package system, but if the project is killed a couple of days after it begins, the company can recoup most of its money. Figure 2 shows the cost of developed systems and package systems over time.

Sometimes, though, it is an advantage to spend the money up front.

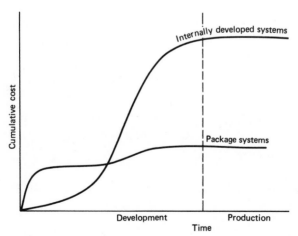

Figure 2. Cumulative cost of systems development.

Implementing a new system is difficult, and people need the proper incentive. When a company sinks $100,000 just to bring a package in the door, it has a real incentive to implement the thing. It is the only way the company can recoup its investment. Thus, with a package, the incentive is to push it through to its conclusion to recoup the investment. With an internally developed system, there is often a strong incentive to stop the project before the investment gets too high.

SUMMARY

Packages have an advantage over internally developed systems in cost, time to implement, and staff required for implementation. Not only this, but the quality and generality of a package is usually superior, and often the company can buy maintenance and enhancements for much lower cost than it could provide them itself. In fact, the only real reason for not selecting a package is if it is not suited to the needs.

REFERENCES

1. Drexel Burnham Lambert, Inc., "Computers: Keys to Productivity in the Eighties," 1980.
2. Electronic System Division, "Summary Notes of a Government/Industry Software Sizing and Costing Workshop," ESD-TR-76-166, 1974.
3. Frederick P. Brooks, Jr., *The Mythical Man-Month*, Addison-Wesley, Reading, MA, 1975.
4. Werner L. Frank, *Computerworld*, September 15, 1980.
5. Bennet P. Lientz and E. Burton Swanson, *Software Maintenance Management*, Addison-Wesley, Reading, MA, 1980.

Chapter 5
What Is a Package?

There is a surprising amount of confusion and naivete about application packages. This is not restricted to the user and financial communities. Data processing people are just as likely to be confused and less likely to realize or admit it.

Most of us are familiar with ready-to-wear or ready-to-use products. Our familiarity with them tends to make us assume that the same ready-to-use attributes apply to software products. In some limited situations this is true, such as for word processors and program development tools. However, with financial application products, if we survive the installation, we will limp away with a wholly different perspective of what ready-to-use means in the package market. This is how data processing people get their scars.

WHO SELLS PACKAGES?

Application products come from a variety of sources and are marketed for a variety of reasons. In the early, unbundled days of the data processing industry, the value and cost of programming was not widely recognized. Consequently, packages of programs were collected, shared, and distributed. However, as the recognition of the dropping ratio of hardware to software cost sank in, a value was attached to these programs and now there is a multimillion dollar industry that develops and sells them.

Much of the early software either was developed by the hardware vendors as a marketing ploy to push iron (their product) or was developed by their clients and licensed back to them for sale and distribution. These products are still in circulation.

The products developed at client sites often are called Field Developed Products or FDPs. They offer the advantage that they were developed in the real world to solve a specific problem. However, they may represent very myopic views of complex problems. Further, they usually are not designed with the intention of sale and distribution, so the control of coding and documentation is generally poor and the packages tend to be hard-wired or specifically engineered rather than parameterized.* Usually these FDP systems are least appropriate for very general applications like payroll, accounts receivable, accounts payable, general ledger and fixed assets. They are more valuable for very specific applications in related industries.

An FDP installment loan system may be a very good product for a bank to purchase because the problem is very specific and was undoubtedly solved by a competitor. It is probably close in function to what the purchasing bank is looking for. On the other hand, a general ledger system developed by the same competitor would be less likely to make a good fit. It will probably be hard-wired with the competitor's chart of accounts, organizational structure, and reports that are unlike those desired by the purchaser.

The hardware vendors do not acquire all their products from clients. They develop many themselves. This is usually done to facilitate the sale of their hardware. As such, the products frequently are offered as loss leaders because of the high margin on hardware sales.

In recent years, hardware vendors have backed away more and more from developing applications software. It is difficult to maintain a staff of experts in financial applications (as you are undoubtedly aware), so they concentrate their effort and resources into developing system software that they must provide.

The applications packages offered by the hardware vendors are more parameterized than the FDPs, they are developed with stricter standards, and they are better documented. However, the products are not necessarily developed by experts in the particular financial disciplines, but rather by expert programmers. Finally, these vendors do not live or die by their application products. They are in the business of developing and selling hardware. If the packages promote these sales, great; if not, the product can be abandoned.

The third source of packages is a group of vendors generally found in the mini-computer market. These vendors offer turnkey systems in which they totally install both hardware and software. Turnkey systems usually are used without data processing staffs.

---

*By parameterized, we mean that values are not hard-wired into programs but are contained in tables or read in as data. For example, a parameterized program would contain the number 50 in a table to represent the number of states, rather than have this value spread around several places in the program. Then when the Carolinas, Dakotas, and Virginias decide to unite, the number 50 in the table can be changed to 47.

The turnkey vendors are almost always operating as Original Equipment Manufacturers (OEMs) for their particular brand of hardware. They make a profit on the hardware, but they are basically pushing hardware to sell software. The systems tend to be well documented from a user's perspective but poorly documented from a data processing perspective. This is because they are stand alone systems that are fed by the user and cared for by the vendor.

For small, discrete applications run on small machines, the turnkey systems are an ideal solution. However, the technical resources of these vendors, which are limited, are allocated long in advance to the development of new products and the enhancement and correction of existing ones. If major modifications or significant technical support are needed for these products, there may be little support or response.

As mentioned before, there is a multimillion dollar software industry that provides generalized financial applications. Most of these vendors are strictly in the business of developing software for major applications on large-scale hardware (typically for IBM OS and DOS environments). Some vendors specialize in only one application while others offer the spectrum of the big five (accounts payable, accounts receivable, personnel/payroll, general ledger, and fixed assets). For solving general problems in large companies, this is the best source. The solutions are very broad (because of the number of clients), very dynamic (because of the competitiveness within the marketplace), and very reliable (because of the large number of users).

WHAT ARE YOU BUYING WITH A PACKAGE?

When a company buys a package, it is paying only a small portion of the development cost of the system. The cost of design, coding of programs, and testing of the product is likely to be 10 to 20 times what is paid. The company is also buying (or avoiding) all of the time it would take to develop and refine such a product. When a company makes a purchase, what will it receive?

Source Code

The package programs should be written in a high level language such as COBOL or PL/I. Insist on this. A product purchased without the source code is dead. At the first instance of error or need for change (even one as simple as increasing a department number from three digits to four), the package succumbs. Changing object code without the source is like trying to work a Rubik's cube in dim light while wearing a catcher's mitt.

The source code along with some of the other items mentioned below arrives on a magnetic tape. Packages have 50,000 to 200,000 lines of source code, and are too large to send on cards.

Object Code

Some vendors provide a compiled version of their software, the object code, along with the source code. This allows a very quick installation of the product in order to begin immediate testing of vendor-supplied data. But since the rest of the system (people, forms, procedures) may not be in place for six months, this immediate installation is of little value.

Sample Job Control Language

The sample Job Control Language (JCL) supplied with packages serves as a good skeleton for data processing people and a source of initial documentation. However, the vendor's job streams must be reconstructed. They may prescribe one edit pass of input data followed by the update phase, while the need may be for several edits in succession before the update. Changes must be made for tape and disk assignments, backups, job libraries, and job accounting information. In short, the JCL provided is a convenient starting point, but it cannot be used as is.

Test Data

Most of the vendors supply test data to prove their system. These data demonstrate a few features of the system without subjecting it to any risk of failure. The data are time worn and well tested. They are trivial, catching only the most obvious installation error, and cannot be relied upon to prove the soundness of the system. The package is not proved until it runs with the company's data.

Documentation

Packages come with a variety of documentation manuals. Some of the vendors provide too much documentation. It will impress the data processing auditor with its bulk, if nothing else. "It weighs 50 pounds," the auditor will say, "Looks like our control problems are finally solved." In practice, its bulk causes control problems. Finding out how things work is like using the *Oxford English Dictionary* to look up a word—an afternoon's adventure. Usually several manuals, intended for different audiences and covering different aspects and perspectives of the package, are provided.

User Manual

The user manual describes the system and how to use it from a clerical point of view. It does not dwell on internal aspects of the system but stresses inputs, outputs, and major functions. Unlike user manuals within your company, it contains no policy or procedures—only the actual workings of the system in fairly sterile terms.

Operations Manual

This document is directed to the computer operations personnel within the data processing group. It describes the flow of the system and the resources (tape, disk, printers, and card readers) required to run it. It also describes any operator interaction, such as forms mounts and responses to console messages. Finally, it describes the job set ups and control cards required to run the package itself. In many installations, this last detail is the responsibility of a data control group who submit jobs to the computer operators for execution.

Systems and Programming Manual

This document is directed toward systems analysts and programmers in the data processing group who will be installing and maintaining (or enhancing) the programs. This document should describe all files as well as the overall system flow and each program. The document may include flowcharts and HIPO diagrams, but most vendors use narratives, which are easier to maintain and update. The manual may also describe possible modifications and how to go about installing them.

Report Writer

Most packages come with a so-called user friendly report writer. They accept requests for reports in a fairly simple language and produce the reports required. This manual may be used by end user and data processor alike. More than one copy will be needed.

Other Manuals

Some packages provide on-line facilities, remote job entry facilities, or data base systems that require additional description. These features are probably described in separate manuals.

Forms

The vendor will supply sample forms (if nowhere else, then as figures in the user manual), and sometimes artwork, layouts, or even acetate overlays. Some of the vendors do a brisk business in selling forms, especially output forms such as payroll registers, payroll and accounts payable checks, and W-2s. They may be reluctant to turn over artwork to a customer for this reason. Without artwork, the input forms must be typeset and pasted up by a professional graphic artist. Get the artwork even if it must be changed.

Training

The vendors normally offer some amount of on-site training. The customer pays travel and expenses. The training usually is divided into three categories—user, systems and programming, and operations— but the customer can decide how the training time is to be spent. Besides on-site training, the vendors hold classes in the major marketing areas (or their home offices) which customers can attend for a reasonable fee. The on-site training is better because the vendor's attention is undivided. However, the classes at the vendor's home base result in an interaction and exchange of ideas from those in other companies that is also beneficial.

Consulting and Hotline

Vendors also offer preinstallation consulting and many have 24-hour hotlines for information. Usually access to these services is for the first year, the typical warranty period. Access after that depends on a maintenance agreement.

Unfortunately, most of the hotline and consulting support is very nontechnical. Many organizations use this position for sales trainees or as a steppingstone into the marketing group. In-depth data processing questions requiring programmer or system analyst skills are filtered through the vendor's bureaucracy before they reach the programming personnel for an answer.

Maintenance

Packages normally come with a one-year warranty. This warranty starts when the source tape is delivered and covers bugs in the program or the inability of the package to perform to specifications. The warranty covers all corrections and enhancements that go into the basic product. It will not cover a newly developed data base module or on-line system that was not a part of the system purchased.

After the first year, ongoing maintenance costs money. Full maintenance runs between 5 and 10% of the original purchase price of the product. It includes all corrections (including corrections to problems identified by other customers) and new releases or enhancements to the basic product. One vendor is currently on the twenty-second release of its general ledger system so the subscription to maintenance can be the assurance that the package does not become obsolete.

Sometimes the maintenance is offered on more than one level. Some companies offer maintenance only, with no enhancement except for legal requirements, such as changes in taxes or mandated reporting. If more than one level of maintenance is offered, full maintenance is best because it keeps the package current. If a company cannot afford the maintenance for a package, it cannot afford the package.

Minor maintenance changes are sent on punch cards or as copies of coding sheets. Only for major revisions or enhancements will the vendor go to the expense of generating the several hundred magnetic tapes necessary to send each customer its changes.

Community of Users and User Groups

One of the big advantages of a package is that it has a community of users. The company benefits by not being the Lone Ranger. Others will locate bugs and lend their voice to demands for enhancements. With a community of users, there is a group to draw upon for experience and even programs or enhancements to programs. Within a large community of users, there is probably a user in the same industry as the company, and the exchange of ideas can be particularly rewarding.

User groups of any size have regular (usually annual) national conventions, and there may be regional meetings and special interest groups as well. These conventions offer instruction and the opportunity to voice concerns and share in the decision of the direction the product will take.

Chapter 6
How Packages Differ
from Development

The installation of an application package and the internal development of a system differ in several important respects. A software package consists of implementing a known solution to an application need. The main consideration is whether there is a match. Developing a system internally consists of designing and building a solution to an application need.

This chapter describes the difference in the system life cycle between a package and an internally developed system. It also describes the difficulties in understanding the internal needs that a package system presents.

LIFE CYCLE COMPARISON

A package can be implemented faster than a developed system. Some vendors claim that their package will be "printing checks in four hours," but this is salesman puffery. It will usually take a year or longer to install a large applications package. A comparable internally developed package might take more than three years, and so the applications package can be installed in roughly a third the time it would take to develop it.

To illustrate the difference, we examine the life cycle of an internally developed system and that of a package implementation. They are significantly different. The system development cycle for internal development is depicted in Figure 3.

Most developed systems follow this curve, within the requirements study, design, programming and debugging, systems testing, installation, and maintenance phases. First we look at the system design phase for an applications package as shown in Figure 4, to see the contrast.

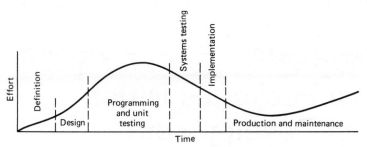

Figure 3.   System life cycle for internal development.

The system life cycle for a package system differs from that of a developed system in several important respects.

Requirements study. This demands more effort in selecting a package because there is less opportunity for customizing or correcting oversights in a package than is possible when designing a system.

Design. A design is not necessary when a package is selected. The system is already designed. Instead, an RFP is written to tell vendors what is wanted. The RFP serves as a means of communicating what is needed to the vendors, and it also serves as a tool for evaluating what they provide.

Programming and debugging. Programming and debugging are not done when a package is bought. Some minor modifications may be needed and some interface and conversion programs may be written, but these represent a small fraction of the total programming effort required.

System test. System testing, which tests the system as a whole,

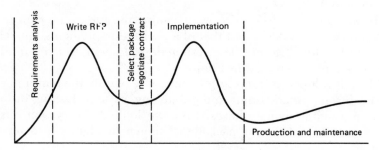

Figure 4.   System life cycle for applications package.

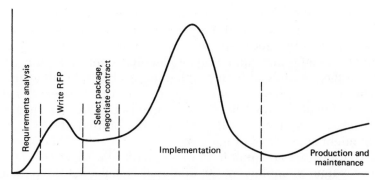

Figure 5.   System life cycle for speeded up applications package.

must be done. The testing must be both with the data provided by the vendor and data prepared by the installation. However, it is less effort than for internal development. There is no equivalent of unit testing, the testing of individual programs, with a package.

Installation. This includes conversion and training. It may require more effort with a package than with an internally developed system because an internal system would probably be customized to handle the current transactions. A package system will probably require all new input forms. Also, a package is less well known than would be an internally developed system. It will be less suited to the specific needs than a custom design.

Maintenance. Since the vendor provides maintenance with a package, there will be less maintenance effort. It will not go away, but it will decrease.

Although the system life cycle for package implementation shows two symmetrical humps, it is the total area beneath the curve that is impor-

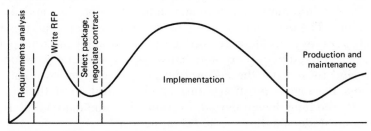

Figure 6.   Systems life cycle for heavily modified applications package.

tant. That is, if the left side is cut down in the selection process, the right side, the implementation, pops up. Figure 5 shows what happens if an attempt is made to speed up the process at the front end. By trying to speed things up, it ends up taking longer. Everything looks good in the schedule at first, but then things begin to fall apart.

The previous graphs assume that there is a fit between what the package provides and what a company needs. If there is not a good fit, the package may have to be modified. If modified, the system life cycle might appear as in Figure 6.

Two things are apparent from these graphs. Packages cost less and take less time to implement than internal systems—if the package is suited to the task. Second, both methods take a considerable amount of time and are difficult.

UNDERSTANDING THE NEEDS

With applications packages, it is far more difficult to understand the needs. We need to examine what this means.

First, what does it mean to understand a system? Before there were computers, people often thought they understood systems. But the computer is a very dumb creature. It takes nothing for granted, it makes no assumptions, and it has no tolerance for ambiguity. Words we use freely to talk to people—"fine," "good," "fairly close," "could be trouble"—have no meaning to the computer. It wants only items that can be quantified. After going through the infinite detail required to design the first computer systems, people realized that the level of understanding they had of systems before the computer was nothing compared to the level of understanding required for computer applications. Computer applications imply the resolution of infinite detail.

Thus, the successful implementation of a computer system is the resolution of infinite detail. It turned out that the design process was just the tool to do this. The designer spent up to a year nailing down each item of information, its format, magnitude, precision, and allowable values. The designer worked closely with the users, and this relationship serves as a catalyst to surface all the strange and unexpected needs that lurked in the corporate hallways. The designer pounded on doors and roused out the accounting people in order to obtain the answers. Posing the questions caused them to think about their needs, and over the long design period, everyone became more comfortable with their understanding of the actual needs.

Programming and debugging were also a learning process. The sys-

tem design was translated into detailed computer language statements, and anything overlooked or inconsistent then surfaced. If
something had been overlooked or needed to be changed, there was
still a chance to do it, although not without cost. The result was that
over the two or three years that it might take to implement the system,
the data processing people and the users developed a very good understanding of the problem.

Now look at what happens with an applications package. There is
no design; it is purchased from the vendor. There is no programming
and testing; that too is purchased from the vendor. There is no catalyst
to get the users to really think about their needs.

As a simple example, consider printing checks in an accounts payable system. Let us take as a starting point that someone wants to print
checks. This sounds easy, but this is only the surface of the problem. It
may turn out that they need to transmit the data to a remote location
and print the checks there. If so, how is the check number that is
printed on a stack of checks in Nome, Alaska sent back to the corporate
offices in say, Dallas, Texas, to include them on the check register and
bank reconciliation?

One must also take into consideration that the printer operator in
Nome, perhaps because of numb fingers, may print about half of a
check run and then jam the printer. Then he will have to discard all
the checks already printed and begin over with a new set of check
numbers. This is neither an easy nor an obvious problem. It is one that
might be surfaced during the design of a system, but how would someone browsing around to select an applications package discover it?

Because there is no design and programming in a package system
and because these are the responsibility of the data processing department, there is much less data processing involvement in the selection
of a package than there is in the design of an internal system. An application package is inherently more of a user system than is an internally developed system. This partially explains the negative reaction
of many data processing people to packages. It reduces their role.

Although data processing has a reduced role with software packages, it is still a major one. It is the role of a service organization, akin
to the use of advertising by the marketing department. Marketing uses
the advertising department to take advantage of technical expertise,
but it does not let advertising develop a marketing plan. Similarly, the
financial departments must use data processing for the technical expertise, but they must not relinquish their responsibilities.

With package systems, the onus for success is far more on the user
departments than it is on data processing. With package systems, the

user departments cannot take the passive view that data processing can get in there and select just the package that will fulfill all their needs. Only the users can do that. And if they are unwilling to do it? Then do not consider a package.

To phrase this differently, the head on the chopping block must be someone from the user department, not data processing. If not, there is little chance of a successful implementation.

With an applications package, the driving force must come from within the user departments. This represents a major reversal from the roles that are usually taken. Usually data processing is aggressive in analyzing needs and the users are passive. With application systems, it is the users who must be aggressive and the data processing department that is likely to be passive.

For example, if the personnel department is buying a system to track people for the company's retirement program, how concerned will a data processing manager be? Tracking people for retirement is not data processing's responsibility. With the rapid turnover of computing people, the data processing manager is not going to retire from the company, nor will anyone who works for him. What do they care about the retirement program? They will care about the payroll program because they receive pay checks, but the retirement program means nothing to them.

We have seen how the system life cycle for an application package differs significantly from internal development. These differences result from the absence of the design and programming that is done for internal development, but the absence of these, especially the design, makes it more difficult for the needs to be known with an applications package.

Chapter 7
What Is Packageable?

There are three broad problem areas suitable for packages: those for system tools, those for programming tools, and those for applications. This chapter discusses these three problem areas and the use of packages for them.

SYSTEM TOOLS

System tools were probably the first packages developed. Early in computing, it became apparent that programmers were solving the same problems repeatedly. Canned solutions quickly developed, many of which were supplied with the hardware by the vendors. Solutions progressed from assemblers, input/output routines, and utilities to primitive batch processors, compilers, linkage editors, and operating systems. Today they are terminal managers and data base systems.

These packages make the hardware usable and efficient. They are the largest and most esoteric programs written, and yet they perform such discrete functions that they are much easier to install than financial application packages. For this reason, we do not treat them extensively in this book.

The life cycle for a system tool is typified by implementation of a new Sort/Merge utility. The utility arrives, on trial, on a magnetic tape containing object code. These products are so jealously guarded that they are rarely distributed in source form.

A systems programmer unloads the object code to a system library and performs some benchmark tests with it. These benchmarks are tests previously run with the old Sort/Merge utility. The purpose of the tests is to verify both that the new Sort/Merge utility produces the same results as the old one and that it runs more efficiently. The vendors make every effort to keep their products compatible. If they do not, even a superior product will not sell because of the effort required to convert to it. Once the benchmarks are validated, the new

Sort/Merge utility is either installed as the standard utility or returned to the vendor.

There are, of course, system tools that require significant effort to convert. The conversion from IBM DOS to OS operating systems is tremendous and requires converting file labels, recompiling and modifying programs, and extensive operator and programmer training. However, these tasks are still discrete to the point that much of the conversion can be programmed on the computer.

There is a host of system tools in data processing centers today, and they represent a significant monthly expense. However, their benefits are fairly quantifiable, and the selection and implementation is usually straightforward, although sometimes difficult.

PROGRAMMING TOOLS

Programming tools form a special case of system tools. They are again large, esoteric programs designed to maximize use of the computer and the productivity of the programmer. These tools include program development tools that allow for on-line entry, update, compilation, and testing of programs. There are also interactive debugging tools, checkout compilers, test data generators, report writers, program generators, documentation systems, and generalized file dump utilities. There is even a special tool called an application generator that is described in Chapter 22.

All of these tools are truly a boon to programming. They are like system tools in that they are fairly discrete, and their impact is quantifiable, at least relative to each other. They are unique in that the end user is a programmer and the installer is a systems programmer. Again, the packages are typically offered on a trial basis so that they are easy to install and evaluate.

APPLICATIONS

Application packages span an imaginative range of task areas. Many are narrowly focused and are omitted from this book. The more general areas are discussed here.

Management

The computer is a tool for converting data into information, and information is the mother's milk of management. The computer is management's monitor of all aspects of the business that can be quantified. Management's primary purpose in obtaining information from the computer is to make decisions.

The computer for management is a decision-making tool, but decision making varies greatly across different organizations and different individuals. Management theory goes in cycles; almost in vogues: centralized, decentralized, theory x, theory y, theory z, and so on. Consequently, generalized management information systems for operating managers have enjoyed no great success. One department may want to look at year-to-date sales; another wants to look at this month's sales compared to the same month last year. One department may be project oriented; another may be organized into skill areas.

Because management's use of computers is so individual, application packages must be in the form of more general tools, such as simulation languages, project control systems, information retrieval packages, data management systems, and data base systems. There are no specific application packages serving management in the same way payroll, general ledger, and fixed assets serve the financial group.

Sales and Marketing

Sales and marketing use the computer much the same as does management—for information upon which to base decisions. The computer can also be used to maintain lists of clients, print sales letters, and log follow-up information. Marketing can make use of statistical packages and use the computer to create and manipulate data bases.

Both sales and marketing are also highly individualized. Two companies marketing the same product might have very dissimilar sales and marketing techniques.

Manufacturing

Manufacturing applications are perhaps more akin to financial applications than are management, sales, and marketing systems. Although there are many ways to do manufacturing, most job shops look remarkably similar, most assembly lines have a common denominator, and parts inventory, reordering, and work in progress translate well from one installation to another.

Manufacturing systems tend to be very complex. Whereas it may take a year to implement a payroll system, it is more likely to take 18 months to implement a manufacturing package.

There is another difference between a manufacturing package and a financial system. Ultimately, a company will get the product manufactured, whether they have a manufacturing system or not. Manufacturing is aided by, but is not totally dependent upon, its computer system. People could still weld, solder, and assemble if there were no computer. This is unlike a payroll or general ledger system for a large company where literally no check would be cut and no accounting product produced without the computer.

Since the computer assists in manufacturing, a manufacturing system can be implemented more gradually. It can also be partially implemented.

Manufacturing is a specialized area. One company specializes in publishing an analysis of manufacturing packages. (See Appendix B.) Manufacturing systems are not covered in this book.

Specific Industries

Each of the specific industries, such as banking, insurance, fast food franchise, airlines, and advertising, has specialized systems developed just for it. Often these systems are developed by one of the companies themselves, rather than by an independent software house. Because these packages are developed for narrow specialties, their functional value overweighs whatever is lost by the package being developed with only one company in mind. These often make excellent systems—if there is a fit. These packages frequently are critical to the business, and in fact, can be the business. A bank, savings and loan, or insurance company could not exist long without specialized packages.

However, because the application areas for specific industries are of interest only to those specific industries, the individual packages will not be covered in this book.

Scientific, Mathematical, Financial Modeling

These packages are usually general purpose in that they depend more on statistics and mathematics than on the particular way a company does business. They tend to be tools of management and engineering. The use of these tools is somewhat akin to programming. Although these tools are getting easier to use, they are often based on FORTRAN, PL/I, APL, or some other programming language. They are often interactive and allow one to manipulate data right at the terminal.

Included in this area also are the data management systems and the small data base systems. Usually interactive, these systems let a person enter their data, select from it, summarize it, do computations, and generate reports. It is difficult to categorize the uses of these systems because they are so broad, ranging from keeping track of employee hours to plotting handicaps of horses. Since they cover a very broad area, they are not described in detail in this book.

Financial

Financial packages, which include personnel/payroll, accounts payable, accounts receivable, general ledger, and fixed assets, are the most general application packages. They all operate under basic accounting rules. As a profession, accountants are perhaps the most standardized, having since the time of the Medici developed their set of generally accepted accounting practices.

These application areas are also heavily regulated, falling under the purview of the SEC, the IRS, ERISA, and more government agencies than it is pleasant to think about. Individuality in financial systems is narrowly restricted. Double entry bookkeeping begins one notch above a child's lemonade stand and is dominant in business thereafter.

With financial applications, the package is the product. There is no payroll in a large company if there is no payroll system to produce it. There is no general ledger without the general ledger system to produce it. They are extremely important systems. No company can exist long without an accounts receivable bringing the cash in, an accounts payable to assure the supply of components, or a payroll system to pay its employees.

People must adhere to a financial application. With a manufacturing system, for example, people might ignore what the system is telling them to do. A foreman might substitute two 50-ohm resistors in series for one 100-ohm resistor if that is what it takes to get the product out the door. There is not this freedom with a financial system. If a payroll check is cut and the information does not get into the payroll file, the general ledger will not balance and the company will probably be fined because the W-2 at year end is incorrect.

Financial systems have discrete elements, such as general ledger numbers or organizational units, that can be quantified. They operate with transactions containing these elements in a standard way, with personnel/payroll, accounts receivable, accounts payable, and fixed assets feeding the general ledger.

These five financial applications have had the most success as standard packages, and it is upon these individual systems that the middle portion of this book focuses.

SUMMARY

Packages for systems tools and programming tools usually are simple to implement and straightforward to use. Their implementation generally takes a short time, often a matter of hours. Application packages involve the participation of many people, and their implementation requires a full-blown project. Systems tools and programming tools can be implemented on a trial basis without a major commitment. Applications packages require a major commitment, and so the requirements analysis and selection for them are far more important.

Chapter 8
How to Look at
a Package

In selecting a package, it is almost as important to know how it works as it is to know what it does. In the following chapters, we look at the major financial applications. For now, though, let us discuss some general considerations that apply to all applications.

To evaluate a package, review each of its major functions, paying close attention to how each is being accomplished. It is like buying a car. A person could enjoy the car without knowing the compression ratio, but a quick peek under the hood that exposed a pair of sweaty mice furiously treading a mill might raise some doubts.

A package should be a natural and appropriate solution to the problem. Does it do what is wanted and does it do it in a practical, natural way? A direct file would be the natural solution for a customer inquiry system. While a package may be able to perform the inquiry with a sequential file, there would be performance problems. When a solution is not natural, there is always a bad side effect.

The operation of most packages revolves around how records are added, changed, or deleted from the master files. There is also a cycle to each system in which normal processing and error correction is done. Look closely at the adjustment cycle. Can adjustments be included with normal processing? Does it require a separate cycle? Can maintenance transactions be included in the normal cycle? Can a separate, off cycle processing be run that accepts only maintenance and adjustments and performs none of the normal cyclical processing? (This is very useful.)

Two events that occur in all systems should be considered in selecting a package: change and growth. Growth occurs both from increase in size and from inflation. Change occurs constantly and the reasons are infinite. One must always think growth and think change in analyzing a package. Other things to look at in a package are the structure and organization of data, the interfaces, and the way the package can be customized. These are described next.

FILE STRUCTURE

There are two ways of collecting data in a system: in a sequential file or in a direct file, usually a data base. In a sequential file system, the records are processed sequentially, with transactions used to update a master file. To process such systems, the entire master file must be read. However, it can be read quickly, and so this type of system is best where most of the master file records are updated each pass. It is relatively fast to update all the records, but relatively slow if only one record is to be updated. As a rule of thumb, if more than 10% of the records are accessed in normal processing, sequential access is faster than direct.

A payroll system epitomizes this. Most employees are paid each pass through the payroll system. But for some companies, this may not be the case. In some states, real estate companies must pay their employees within three days after closing a sale. Movie companies must pay their extras daily.

The other type of file is a direct file. It permits individual records to be updated. For a physical analogy of a sequential file, visualize a paymaster at an army base. The equivalent of a sequential file would be to line up all the soldiers on payday and have them march by, handing each of them their pay as they passed. This would be the fastest way if everyone got paid. With a direct file, the paymaster would call out the name of each soldier and have each step forward to be paid. This would be the fastest way if only a few soldiers got paid.

A direct file permits individual records to be updated. In financial application systems, most direct files are used to form a data base system. One of the main advantages of data base systems is that the relationship of things can be recorded as data. A data base could show the relationship between people, departments, and projects. People belong to certain departments and work on certain projects. By preserving this relationship in a data base, people can query it. They might ask to which department a person belongs and who the other people are in the department. Or they could ask which other projects are being worked on by the people within the department. This can also be done with a sequential file, but only in the batch mode, and only by reading the entire file. By contrast, the relationship in a data base allows one to query it from a terminal with very quick response.

For example, with a sequential file, if someone wanted to see all the employees within a department, they would submit a batch job to sort the file and select the people who are in the department. They might get their answer a few hours later. With a data base system, they could ask the system to list all those employees in a particular department and get them displayed on their terminal in seconds.

Data base management systems are generally large and expensive—larger and more expensive than financial packages. Consequently, financial packages are not built as data base management systems. They are also not built to depend on existing data base management systems because the vendors do not want their packages predicated upon the use of another vendor's data base system. However, some vendors build their application packages to have some of the characteristics of data base management systems by taking a data base approach in their design.

The data base approach represents the leading edge of technology. However, it does have drawbacks. In application packages based on the data base approach, a record or bucket is created to accommodate the data, such as a bucket for each general ledger account for a department. (There are other ways of doing this, but most application packages do it this way.) This can result in monstrous files for some applications. Suppose data is to be accumulated by general ledger numbers and departments, and there are 100 departments and 1000 general ledger numbers. This file would need 100,000 buckets. If each department used about 5 general ledger numbers, only 500 of the 100,000 buckets would be used.

This would be expensive and wasteful because to add up all the general ledger amounts would involve looking at 100,000 buckets to add only 500 numbers. In one company, this resulted in a system increasing in run time from 2 hours to 17. It is a good illustration of an application not matching a package.

A data base also allows different data to be tied together so that when one item is updated, another item gets updated too. If an accounting system were made a data base, a payroll transaction could update the personnel/payroll record for each employee and also update the general ledger account.

The disadvantage of data bases is that such systems are an order of magnitude more difficult to maintain. They also consume vast amounts of computer time and disk space if used improperly. There is not enough experience yet to tell what will happen should someone ever want to replace them. It will undoubtedly be much more difficult than replacing a sequential file system.

PERIPHERAL ISSUES

Few systems are implemented that truly stand alone. Possibly the current wave of video games represents the only exception. Nearly all application systems either feed on other systems, are fed by other systems, or both.

Consider personnel/payroll. A timekeeping system may feed it. It will certainly feed general ledger, and will probably feed a labor or project reporting system, a retirement system, and a check reconciliation system. It may also feed an Employee Stock Ownership Plan (ESOP) system and an Electronic Funds Transfer (EFT) system. These are just the common examples. Every company has its own peculiar systems.

One of the most important things to look at in a system are interfaces—the ports of entry and exit provided by the system. Unfortunately, the term interface is overused to the point where not only machine parts interface, but people, pets, documents, and even governments do, too. When the accountant says that accounts payable and general ledger do not interface, what does he mean? It could be that none of the data entered into accounts payable is ever passed to the general ledger. This, we would all agree, would mean that accounts payable does not interface with general ledger.

Far more likely, however, is that accounts payable does pass data to general ledger, but there are limitations on what is passed. Maybe accounts payable does not carry the proper account numbers, or the reconciling cash entry is not properly posted. Probably the accounts payable distribution line item account numbers are not validated in general ledger. Thus accounts payable may accept data and disburse funds against accounts that general ledger considers invalid. This is not so much a lack of interface as a lack of integration.

For our purposes, we will consider that two systems are interfaced if a bridge exists between them that allows data to be passed without manual intervention. We will define integration to mean that the path between the two systems is two way and the systems cannot run if disconnected. That is, one system can send data to another, and the second system must examine the data, send it back, or send other data back before the first system can continue.

Typically, application systems are interfaced rather than integrated. They are designed to run stand-alone, but are capable of producing interface files that connect two or more applications together. Interfaced systems are easier to install, maintain, and test than integrated systems because problems can be isolated and handled separately. Any connection or interface is discrete and is probably contained within a single file.

Unfortunately, the ultimate goal is not an interfaced system, but an integrated one. When an employee's department number is changed, the new number should be verified within the general ledger organization table or file. Similarly, when a voucher is input to accounts payable, the distribution accounts and organizations should be verified in general ledger.

Because of the problems of interface and integration, several vendors highlight the fact that they offer a family of integrated packages. They argue that one should stick with a single vendor for all packages to avoid interface problems, maintain consistency between the packages, and earn a price discount (from 10 to 25%) in addition. This argument will appeal to the purchasing agent, if he is still involved in the package selection. "Hey, those guys are ready to deal. I can swing a 25% discount if we get the whole ball of wax from one vendor." The purchasing agent has found his means of evaluation—price. Never mind that the package might not fit.

These arguments have some holes. If the packages were truly integrated and not just interfaced, the arguments might hold. However, the packages are often designed by different teams of people, and bear little resemblance to each other, outside of the covers and logos on the documentation. Because they are designed to be sold and run independently, they share little more interface than a simple transaction file.

A vendor may boast an integrated accounts payable/general ledger system that validates accounts payable transactions against general ledger accounts and organizations. The catch is that these general ledger accounts and organizations are not the ones stored in the general ledger system but are in a separate file that someone must maintain for accounts payable. This means that someone must remember to enter a transaction to update this accounts payable file every time an account is added, changed, or deleted in the general ledger system. Inevitably, the files will get out of synchronization. Make sure that the vendor explains exactly how the package does its interfacing.

Most interfaces are, in fact, just interface files. The interface of payroll, accounts payable, fixed assets, and accounts receivable to general ledger usually consist of journal vouchers (JVs). While the format of JVs from one vendor's payroll is different from that expected by another vendor's general ledger, the differences are minor. After all, a JV is a JV is a JV. This transaction, regardless of vendor, carries a transaction code, date, description, amount, debit/credit code, account number, and organization. The field sizes and their order may differ, but these are only minor reformatting problems as long as the content is there.

Reformat programs to convert transactions from one format to another can be written and tested by junior programmers in a few days. If there is a content problem, such as an accounts payable JV file that does not carry an organization code, the account number must be looked up in a table. The program could then take a few days longer to write and test. The point is that the concern should be with getting the best package for an individual application (provided the interface is sufficient), and not the best family of packages for all applications.

SIGNIFICANT ELEMENTS

The records in an application have fields predefined as necessary for most of the application needs. Someone needs to determine if they are present and if they can contain the data needed. If a payroll were implemented for the British Royal Family and the name field was limited to 30 characters, Charles Philip Arthur George Mountbatten, Prince of Wales, Windsor would cause some problems.

Several data elements appear in all the financial packages, and in fact, most application packages. Each of these is explained in detail.

Account/Organization/Project Identification

Most financial systems require three items of information to properly collect costs: a general ledger acount number, an organizational unit such as a department or group number, and a project or job number. These three items are the heart of most financial systems.

Account Number

All companies have a chart of accounts, and most transactions have an associated general ledger account number. The account number is usually hierarchical. All the different travel accounts may be grouped to form a total travel cost, and travel may be grouped with hotel costs to analyze convention expenses. The account number also has attributes, such as direct or indirect, asset or liability, and expense or revenue.

Organization

A transaction usually applies to a specific unit within an organization. In a cost system, an employee belongs to some department and does work for some department. Usually they are the same department, but not always. Consequently, there is sometimes a need to record two organizations for cost transactions; the organization supplying the cost item and the organization to be charged with the cost. The organization is inherently hierarchical.

Project or Job Number

The job number tells what the cost was incurred for, and is a means of collecting costs for both billing purposes and to aid management. Most organizations have some form of job costing system. The job number collects costs for projects, locations, and activities. The job number often is hierarchical. In a project-oriented system this allows a contract to be broken up into work orders, projects, and tasks for costing, and then the costs can be aggregated to various levels for reporting.

Hierarchy

The hierarchy is the way in which accounts, organizations, or projects are subdivided. A heirarchy is needed to be able to assign costs to the proper level, to generate totals, and to aggregate them to higher levels.

Suppose an organizational hierarchy was composed of group, department, and division. The need would be to aggregate all the group costs to the department level, and all the department costs to the division level. But there may also be a need to charge the costs to any level—perhaps some costs to a group level, but other costs directly to the division level. This would save having to define a dummy group to capture costs at the division level.

The first consideration is the number of hierarchical levels permitted. There should be room to add more levels as the company grows and reorganizes. The highest level is usually the corporate level to enable the system to handle several legal entities for which the parameters, account structure, calendar, and policy differ.

The next item to consider is the length of the field allowed to specify the level. If there is a seven-digit organization code for each unit in a company, it would cause unending problems to install a package that allowed only five digits.

Another consideration is whether the three items, account, organization, and project, are treated independently in the system. Does the system permit the three to be defined individually, or is one considered to be the part of the hierarchy of another? For example, some packages make the account the level below the organization. That works well for some companies, but is entirely wrong for others.

Attributes

With each of the three entities, account, organization, and project, some attributes are needed. There are different ways of assigning attributes in a coding scheme. One way is to build the attributes into the numbers themselves. For example, account numbers 001 through 199 might be assets and 200 through 499 might be liabilities. This makes it easy to tell from its number whether an account is an asset or liability. The problem with this is there are never enough numbers and it does not allow for multiple attributes. Perhaps other attributes, such as direct or overhead, must be attached to the account number. The best way to assign attributes is through a table. This does not preclude assigning ranges of numbers for asset or liability, or expense or revenue, to make the account numbers have more meaning. Assigning ranges of numbers also makes it easier to generate reports with a report writer. Report writers like to operate on ranges of account numbers.

Coding Schemes

When setting up a coding scheme, such as one for part numbers, the codes can serve to define the item. For example, if a code were made up for mouthwash, the first two digits might indicate the size of the bottle, the third the color, the fourth the flavor, and the last two the price. Selecting codes that are readily understood by the people using them reduces error. For example, a part number of 30YK79 could be easily recognized as a 30 ounce bottle of yellow colored, kumquat flavored mouthwash priced at 79 cents—in other words, you basic 79-cent kumquat mouthwash.

The advantage of including attributes as part of the coding scheme is that the coding by itself can convey many of the attributes without reference to other sources. When the user of the code needs this information, including it as part of the coding scheme is very convenient. The problem with codes comes when the attributes that are built into the code can change. Yellow will still be yellow next year, but a 79-cent bottle of mouthwash is likely to be $3.85. Where the attributes can change, they should be given arbitrary values as table references. The price would have been better if coded as 02, and the 02 used as a reference to a table in which the current price is stored. Price, of course, should never be built in as an attribute.

Accounting Cycle

The solar system has not been kind to the accountant. The fact that the measurment of a day, one spin of the earth, is unrelated to the measurement of the year, the passage of the earth around the sun, results in a calendar not at all amenable to the cold logic of the computer.

The 365 or 366 days in a year are also unfortunate numbers because they are not evenly divisible into anything useful. The month, which is based on the movement of the moon, works well as an accounting period because there are exactly 12 months in a year, and 12 is evenly divisible by 2 or 4 for semiannual or quarterly aggregations. However, the next division, the week, is unrelated to the month. Now it gets messy.

Unless the company can convince its employees to live on a single paycheck a month, a semimonthly, biweekly, or weekly pay period is selected. If semimonthly, the end of a pay period falls on arbitrary days of the week, which makes scheduling a nightmare. If based on the week, the pay periods fall arbitrarily within the month, and all months will not contain the same number of pay periods. Since this distorts accounting reports, a four-week accounting period is often used, with a weekly or biweekly payroll.

But now the accounting periods do not exactly fit a year. If a company has a biweekly payroll and a four-week accounting period, the 13 accounting periods in a year contain only 364 days. Furthermore, the 13 accounting periods do not divide evenly for semiannual or quarterly reporting. The usual solution is to establish something like, 4, 3, 3, 3 accounting periods per quarter, and not worry that one quarter is longer than the others and that the two semiannual periods are unequal.

History

When data are not summarized, the accounting period is not particularly troublesome. To report for an accounting period, a quarter, or semiannually, one need only select the detailed transactions that fall within these periods, whatever they happen to be.

When data are summarized, the problem becomes acute. For example, if a report is to show year-to-date, quarter-to-date, and current period amounts, a file may have to be designed to contain the information, and the relationship between the pay period, accounting period, quarter, and year may dictate the layout of the record. A subsequent requirement for month-to-date information is then not just a simple report request; it might mean that a new file must be designed.

Data, especially management data, usually mean more when compared with other data. Current period sales, for example, have more meaning when compared to the sales of the past three periods or of the same period last year. This is especially true in spotting trends and in analyzing the effect of management decisions. If a company's business is seasonal, then historical data are almost a necessity for making any meaningful comparisons.

Another problem in comparisons with historic data is that there is a conversion from the old system to the new system. The new system may contain data to a different level of detail. The company may also change its entire coding structure in implementing a new system if the old coding structure was antiquated. Account, job, and department numbers are the most likely to change. The data for the new system may not be available at the same level of detail. This is a price that a company pays for changing it accounts and its organization. It needs to be considered in any implementation.

If the historical data are more detailed than the data for a new system, they can be aggregated by using a table that maps the old data to the new data. If three accounts in the last year's data become a single account in this year's data, the three accounts of last year can be looked up in a table to convert them to this year's account. But if it goes the other way, so that the current data are more detailed than the historical data, this does not work. If one account last year becomes three accounts this year, a fixed percentage can be allocated to each, it can all be allocated to one of this year's accounts, or it can be allocated manually.

Dates

Several dates often must be carried in a single transaction: the date the transaction originated, the date of booking (the effective date of the accounting transaction), the date of entry (when it is entered into the computer), and the date of processing. These dates are important for the audit trail and for validation and program logic. For example, the booking date can be compared to the accounting period end date to ensure that current transactions are being processed.

There are two common forms of dates, calendar and julian. Calendar dates are of the form mm/dd/yyyy, although the European convention is to write the date as dd/mm/yyyy. Julian dates are of the form yyyy.ddd, where ddd is the sequential day of the year, 1 to 366. The advantage of the julian date is that it is easier to compute the number of days between two dates. The disadvantage is that people are more familiar with calendar dates.

Two digits for the year may seem adequate, but many packages selected today will still be running at the turn of the century. Then the sort on date is going to cause all kinds of problems because a two-digit year will go from 99 to 00. Look for systems that carry the year as four digits.

The comparison of dates gets confusing if they are stored in mm/dd/yyyy or dd/mm/yyyy format. Using a report writer to select everyone who was hired prior to 06/01/1975 requires that the date be dissected and resequenced for the comparison (1975/06/01) or a complicated, nested comparison, of the year, then month, and then day must be used. It is better to carry the date internally in yyyy/mm/dd form and then reformat it for output to reports.

Dollar Amount

Dollar amounts should be carried in dollars and cents, even if only whole dollars are to be reported. Cents are often needed for accuracy in forming totals, or a new report may require showing dollars and cents.

Often debits and credits are carried as separate fields in records in order to balance the debits and credits. Even when debits and credits are carried separately, the dollar amounts should be signed.

Hours

The conventional measurement of time in hours and minutes is inconvenient to use as data in the computer. Instead, time is usually carried in hours and fraction of hours. The minimum measurement of time in most situations is the minute, and two decimal places is sufficient for this. Fractional hours should be carried to two decimal places so that there is capability of being accurate to the minute.

When time is filled in by hand, there is a question of whether to enter it in hours and minutes and convert it to fractional form inside the computer, or to enter time on the source input in fractional form. Should a person fill in 8 hours, 15 minutes, or 8.25 hours on a timesheet? Ultimately it does not matter all that much because people can adapt to either.

Descriptions

An extremely important but frequently ignored item of information to be included in a source transaction is a description or comments field. The description field allows the user to comment on the transaction. For correcting entries especially, the description may later prove valuable as part of the audit trail.

Names

A person's name is composed of three parts, a first name, a middle name (or just the initial), and a last name. (In other countries, people can have several more names that make each person a walking genealogical chart.) The name fields should be alphanumeric. The following field sizes for names are suggested:

Last name—18 characters. According to the *Guiness Book of Records*, Featherstonehaugh is the longest English name. Allow an extra character for the joker who wants to get in the *Guiness Book of Records*. With the current vogue of hyphenated names (Fawcett-Majors), even 18 characters may not be enough.

First name—12 characters. Christabelle is the longest of the common given names.

Middle name—18 characters. The middle name is often a family name.

In addition to the name, there may be titles: Mr., Mrs., Ms., General, and The Right Honorable are prefixes; Jr. and Esq. are frequent suffixes. Room should be allowed for these if necessary.

Since the name will probably be used in a sort and be printed, the name will often be carried twice, once for printing and once for sorting. This saves having to write a program to format names for printing.

Addresses

An address is usually composed of the following:

Person's name (optional)
Company name (optional)
Division name (optional)
Street address and room, suite, or apartment number
City, state, zip code
Country (optional)
Foreign postal code (optional for Canada, Australia, West Germany, and a growing number of countries)

If city or state will be sorted upon, they must be separate fields in the file. The following field sizes are suggested:

Company name—50 characters. However, this will require abbreviating The Bank of America National Trust & Savings Association. International Minerals & Chemical is the longest of the *Fortune 500* names.

Division name—50 characters. Same as the company name.

Street address—Allow two lines of 40 characters. This allows some extra for the number and room, suite, or apartment number.

City—23 characters. If Southampton Long Island can be contained, other names should fit too.

State—14 characters if spelled out. This accommodates the Carolinas. Two characters if the Postal Service code for state is used.

Zip Code—Nine characters. (Going up from 5—maybe. Canada currently has 6 characters in its zip. Foreign zip codes are often kept as a separate field.)

Country—18 characters. Dominican Republic is the longest name not usually abbreviated. Allow 26 characters to include The People's Republic of China, 37 characters if the Democratic People's Republic of Yemen (and Korea) is on a mailing list, and 38 characters for the longest name of a member of the United Nations; Byelorussian Soviet Socialist Republic.

CUSTOMIZATION

Almost all packages require some customization. The packages provide several means of customizing the package that do not destroy the integrity of the package or interfere with the vendor's updating it.

User-Defined Exits

Package vendors know that they cannot provide everything that any user might need. To get around the problem, they provide user exits. There are two key considerations in evaluating the user exits:

> Are the user exits at the appropriate place? If a user exit is needed to modify some data that are to go into the calculation of a person's salary, a user exit that is given control after the salary is calculated does no good.
> Are the data available at the user exit? Again using the payroll example, since some data must be changed before calculating a salary, a user exit that does not give access to the needed data does no good.

User-Defined Fields

The system should provide for user-defined fields in files. There must be enough fields and they must be large enough.

Check Handling

Check handling is a very complicated problem, as we shall see. There must be some method of reconciliation. There must be some way to void checks. If they are voided, there should be a way to reverse the check by check number. On a payroll check, for example, if a check cannot be voided and reversed by check number, someone must enter transactions to back out not only the face value of the check, but all the payroll deductions and any other information that was affected by the check.

There must be a provision for handwritten checks. Two things are required: a way of stopping the system from producing the check and a way of getting the information on the handwritten check into the system.

Finally, checks must be printed. Even this has its complications. If an accounts payable system is run for different companies in a corporation, each may have its own bank account and its own check stock. It is best to have the checks for each account come out as a separate print file to aid the operators in mounting the proper check stock.

The biggest problem in printing checks is to get the physical check number on the check into the system so it prints on the check register. This is not easy. One way is to have the operator tell the system the beginning check number at the start of the check print cycle. Then the system can save this number internally, and it will match the number preprinted on the checks for reconciliation. The problems come about if the printer jams or messes up some checks. Is the check print program rerun, giving it a new number?

This problem is even worse when check data are transmitted to a remote location for printing. Then what happens if the operator has to reprint the checks?

Another way of handling the problem is to print the check number on the check itself with the check writing program. This requires a special printer because the check number that appears in the upper right hand part of a check is also printed at the bottom of the check in MICR code.

The final way of handling this problem is to print a pseudo-number on the check, and then have the operator record the range of physical check numbers that correspond to the pseudo-numbers. This information must then be fed back into the system so that the check register can look up the check number from the pseudo-number. It is not an easy problem.

We have now covered the general aspects of application packages. The next several chapters describe each of the five major financial packages: personnel/payroll, accounts payable, accounts receivable, general ledger, and fixed assets. These chapters are technical, and you may want to read only the chapters in which you have a particular interest.

Chapter 9
Personnel/Payroll
Packages

PAYROLL VERSUS PERSONNEL

Payroll accounting was a candidate for automation long before the current spate of government- and management-mandated personnel reports arrived. As a result, even though payroll and personnel are closely related they are often implemented as two separate systems.

In most organizations the payroll and personnel functions are performed in separate departments. Considerable time is spent in communicating, resolving discrepancies, coordinating hires and terminations, and maintaining redundant records. The same is true of automated payroll and personnel systems when they are implemented as separate entities.

Because of the extent and sensitivity of personnel/payroll information, the two people functions should be separate. There is no reason for a payroll clerk in a large organization to be privy to an employee's medical history. By the same token, there is no reason for a benefits clerk processing medical claims to know an employee's salary. There is a good deal of overlap, however, between the two functions, and they must be well coordinated. Payroll must be aware of new employees, terminations, and salary increases as personnel makes them. Personnel should be aware of the vacation, holiday, and sick hour reporting done through payroll.

While it is a good idea to separate the payroll and personnel groups, it is a bad idea to separate the two systems or files. Companies that have separate systems with separate files have constant headaches in coordinating the two. Both systems must be maintained and updated consistently.

If there are two systems, it is almost certain that data in the two systems will become inconsistent. One solution is to have all payroll input drive the personnel system. In this way, any transactions entered for payroll are also entered into personnel. However, personnel may wish to retain individual records that payroll does not care about, such as terminated employees. Consequently, personnel may not delete records that are deleted in the payroll file. Now the two files are inconsistent.

Undoubtedly there are more elaborate solutions to the problems of maintaining two separate systems, but the solutions are just that— elaborate. They will also be difficult to maintain. The best solution is to have one system and one file.

Package vendors view payroll and personnel as closely related functions, but most modularize their packages. Some offer separate files, but most use a single file with separate functions. That is, the payroll check writing function is separate from the EEO reporting function and either can be run independently of the other.

When replacing either a payroll or personnel system, consider doing both. It is easier to do both together than each separately. More than half the data in payroll and personnel are shared, and the whole process, machine and manual, is simplified by using one system.

GENERAL PERSONNEL/PAYROLL PACKAGE APPROACH

Nearly all of the major personnel/payroll packages on the market today take a similar approach to processing. They differ in the way they are implemented and on their internals, but the approach is basically the same.

Master Files

The basic approach calls for a sequential master file. (On-line packages may have an indexed sequential file or even a data base.) The master file is processed in chunks called companies, groups, paygroups, organizations, or corporations. This is done according to sets of parameters that define the payroll and benefit characteristics for each entity. These parameters may be maintained in a separate file, in a table, or even on a series of control cards. The most popular approach is to include them on the master file itself. Each group of employees is preceded by records that define the characteristics of that group.

Processing

As each group is encountered, the parameters are loaded into memory to direct the processing for the group. Usually the groups are treated as autonomous units. The payroll cycles, schedules, earnings, and deduction types differ for each group. Package users include large service bureaus and bank processing centers whose clients are autonomous and must be treated so. This is also a convenient feature for multidivisional and multinational companies where the characteristics of a payroll differ greatly between the corporate offices and the plants where the bargaining units reign.

The input to the payroll system includes transactions for adding new employees, changes to existing employees, terminations, leaves of absence, and actual payments and adjustments. Most systems allow any of these to be submitted in a single cycle of the system. This is very convenient because employees may be hired, paid, and terminated in a single cycle. To stretch this out over several cycles gets confusing.

Pay Types

The pay input also includes transactions for time cards, job tickets, adjustments, and similar items. Most packages recognize several pay statuses for employees:

1. Time card (hourly wage) employees. These employees are paid only for hours worked. No time card—no pay. Hours entered on time cards are multiplied by the wage stored on the employee record. There may be a provision for an override of hourly wage on the time card, which is very useful.

2. Salaried employees. These employees are paid a fixed salary on a weekly, biweekly, semimonthly, or monthly basis, without the need for time card input. Time cards may be input in some systems to record labor or for project accounting but usually input is given only for bonuses or to record leave without pay or sick time. Company policy may dictate that sick pay is the same as full pay, but it is important to input this time separately and calculate pay for it separately, because the income is generally not subject to FICA tax, to state disability tax, and to federal and state unemployment taxes (FUI and SUI).

3. Exception time card/exception hourly employees. This is a special classification of employee done for convenience in

large systems. The category may not exist in the company, but in fact it is possible and often desirable to classify all employees in this way.

Typically, the exception pay people are treated as if they were hourly or time card individuals—with one major distinction. While their pay is stored in their record as an hourly wage, they are paid automatically a fixed number of hours if no time card is input for them. If a time card is input, then they are paid only for hours input on the time card, or, in some packages, these hours are paid and then subtracted from the normal hours to be paid before normal pay is computed. This "exception hourly pay" method can duplicate both time card and salary pay, and has several advantages:

Exception hourly pay accumulates the hours worked needed for ERISA vesting and eligibility calculations. Salary pay does not accumulate hours.

Exception hourly pay supplies hours to a labor or project accounting system. Salary pay supplies only dollars.

Deduction of lost time from paychecks is automatically calculated based on hours away from the job. One need only submit an exception hourly timecard and let the system calculate pay. This is also true for sick time, which should be entered separately, even though gross pay is not affected.

The pay calculation is consistent for everyone.

There are also some disadvantages:

Most companies view employees as hourly or salaried, and they want to see them reported this way. Companies are comfortable seeing skilled labor reported in hourly rates, but they generally do not quote salaries of salesmen, accountants, or executives in terms of dollars per hour. Such salaries are presented in dollars per month or year. This can cause problems.

If all employees are exception hourly, a separate code must indicate whether they are hourly or salaried and nonexempt or exempt, in order to report their compensation correctly. With this code, a report can calculate a monthly or yearly salary and print this instead of the hourly wage carried in the file. This salary may not exactly equal the actual salary offered to potential employees or recorded in salary increase notices. The discrepancy, due to rounding or truncation errors in converting from monthly salary to hourly wage, is only a few cents. That is, a monthly salary of $1800.00 might be quoted. But this might come out to $1799.97 per month when converted to an hourly rate.

Most employees think of wages in dollars per hour and salaries in dollars per month. If salaries are converted to dollars per hour, employees will be upset when they see the result of penny round off errors on their pay checks. There is a simple solution to this. Give the employees a $0.0001 per hour raise when they are hired. This will cost the corporation a maximum of $0.21 a year per employee (plus the attendant FICA, FUI, and SUI), but it will eliminate the complaints. In addition, in notifying employees of their salary, give them the actual rate per hour, per pay period, and per year to avoid any confusion. This may cause some employees minor emotional problems when they see their salary quoted as an hourly rate, but stress to them that the hourly wage input to the system is strictly for more precise accounting.

Because of salary rounding problems, the hourly wage field must give four or more decimal places of precision. Also, many union contracts call for hourly wages with fractional cent rates, such as $10.375 per hour.

EDITING OF PERSONNEL/PAYROLL DATA

Editing of personnel/payroll input is performed in three steps. The first two steps are done in an edit phase, and the third step is done in the compute phase.

The edit, which includes syntax editing of the data, is done without reference to the master file. However, it may use tables of acceptable values, such as department and account numbers. These syntax edits validate that the input transactions have the correct format, that salaries and wages are numeric and fall between acceptable ranges, that necessary fields are present, and that certain fields contain only accepted values, such as "M" or "F" for sex.

Editing is critical for packages. Certain fields may drive special processing that the installation requires. If the data are not edited when they go into the system, the results produced cannot be depended upon. These results include reports and analyses critical to the operation of companies.

Besides the syntax editing, there is a validation edit. Sometimes this edit is not a part of a separate edit phase but is included in the compute phase. Validation editing verifies that an employee in an input transaction exists in a master file, and that an employee added to the file does not already exist in the file.

The most complicated edit occurs when an employee is transferred from one position in the file to another. This is complex because two locations on the master file must be accessed to verify that the employee exists now and also that his or her new location is not already occupied by an existing employee. This is handled in two ways. One way is to explode the transfer into two transactions and edit them separately. The other way is to delay the test for the new location of the employee until the compute phase.

Some errors cannot be identified until the compute phase. These errors include deductions not taken (not enough net pay is left over), overflowing limits (a FICA deduction is input that causes a total withholding of more than the FICA limit), or running negative balances on earnings (at the beginning of a quarter a void check is input for an employee with no offsetting earnings). In addition to these computation errors, there are other errors that are more conveniently caught in the compute phase. A time card input for a terminated employee could be caught in the validate portion of the edit, but it is easier to catch it in the compute phase because most packages allow the status for any employee to be changed several times during the cycle.

The package vendors recommend that only the edit phase be run until all errors are corrected. Since some errors can be caught only in the compute phase, this works only in theory. After several iterations of the edit, there may still be some errors. Many companies adopt a different approach in installing a package. They run a full edit and compute in order to catch all of the errors. If there are no significant errors to justify a rerun, then the output of the compute is accepted. If there are serious errors, the input transactions are corrected and the edit and compute are rerun. This is the best way to do editing if one has the luxury of the additional computer time necessary.

USER TABLES

One of the most exciting developments of the modern personnel/payroll packages is the user table facility. In any company, there are many tables that are maintained to keep track of department numbers, project numbers, product numbers, EEO classifications, job codes, account numbers, and many other codes and classifications. Usually these tables contain descriptions as well as the codes themselves. Thus department number 100 may carry the description OFFICE OF THE PRESIDENT, which is used for reporting.

An individual table can serve multiple purposes. Consider the department number table. The numbers are probably used by the existing payroll system to validate department numbers on time cards. They may also be used by the general ledger system to verify department numbers on journal voucher transactions. The descriptions accompanying the department numbers are probably printed on labor reports, project accounting reports, and personnel reports.

The early packaged systems allowed codes and other information to be stored on the master file. However, they did not provide convenient ways to enter these data into tables. With the move to integrating personnel/payroll systems, most of the vendors now provide user-defined tables in their packages. Many codes and data elements can now be stored in these tables. The items stored might include:

EEO code
EEO job code
Union
Job classification
Machine code (drill press, lathe, etc.)
Shift code
Langauge skill (Spanish, German, French, etc.)
Degree (BA, BS, MS, PhD, etc.)
University
Job skills
Employee classification (executive, manager, clerical, etc.)
Department number
Division number

The edit should use these tables to validate the codes on personnel/payroll transactions. Failing this, the report writer should access the tables in order to infer the description for printing reports.

The tables should be stored in some indexed sequential format (in IBM terminology either ISAM or VSAM) so that the tables can be accessed sequentially or randomly. In addition, access to the tables should be easy because other programs will need to use these tables.

USER-DEFINED DATA

No matter how much thought goes into the design of a packaged system, it is impossible to conceive of all of the personnel data that a company may need to carry in the master file. For example, a package system may have a field for job classification that will adequately carry a company's job classification structure, but the company may need separate job classifications to report data to an external agency, such as Department of Defense or salary compensation surveys. Or a package may carry a field for spouse's first name but have no field for the spouse's social security number or last name.

The vendors make an effort to define all of the data elements they can think of, including many that are not applicable to all companies. This allows them to define input transaction formats and generate a multitude of reports with the report writers. However, the vendors recognize that they cannot think of every possibility and they certainly lack the prescience to anticipate future governmental requirements. They therefore provide users with the ability to define additional fields that can be input, updated, and reported.

Look closely at these fields and the restrictions that the vendor places on their definitions when selecting a package. Some vendors have a set number of fields with fixed formats. For example, there may be 26 eight-character fields into which codes, dates, or other alphanumeric data can be stored. There may also be a limited number of fields for numeric data. This type of implementation is weak because it does not give true user-defined fields but rather a set of vendor-defined fields that can be used.

A better approach, adopted by several vendors, is to reserve a user space on the master file record containing several hundred characters. This space can be defined by the user into individual fields of varying lengths and formats. This offers the greatest latitude and the best chance that a package will accommodate the changing needs.

The user-defined data in a package should include the following features:

1. Edit of input.
2. Definition of field length.
3. Definition of field format.
4. Access to the field from the report writer.

5. Access to the field from the compute and update phases.
6. External dictionary definition of the field.

These items need to be described in detail.

Edit of Input

To be of any use, the field being defined must be edited to assure some confidence in its contents. When these fields are defined, there should be a way to request editing that the package already uses, such as a standard date edit or a numeric edit. There should also be a way to program in other editing.

Some systems allow edits to be defined for fields by expressing the edits as parameters in tables. For example, one could define an edit for sex as being equal to "M" or "F." Similarly, an edit for marital status may be "S" (single), "M" (married), "D" (divorced), or "W" (widowed). Table edits usually allow a range of values to be specified as well. For example, insurance coverage may be $10,000 to $100,000. Table edits are handy because they are installed without programming, and they are self-documenting. A listing of a table can be included in the user manual in an appendix to define valid data.

Some implementations of the table edits are weak. The weaknesses include:

The inability to edit more than a limited number of characters. (One vendor allows only six characters to be specified.)
The inability to specify more than one range of values for a field. (For a certain datum, the valid ranges may be 1 through 5 and 10 to 15.)
The inability to specify more than one edit.

Definition of Field Length

The length of any field should be as long as needed. If a vendor arbitrarily defines x number of 1-character fields and y number of 6-character fields, space will be wasted in some cases and fields will be too short in others. As a rule of thumb, the field lengths should allow for fields ranging from 1 to 18 characters.

Definition of Field Format

One should be able to specify fields as numeric or alphanumeric. For numeric, the decimal places should also be specified. These requirements can be circumvented but only with effort. Packages should allow things to be done naturally. Also, arithmetic is faster if numeric data are stored as numeric.

Access to the Field from the Report Writer

Often the reason a field is added to the file is to display it on reports. For example, job classification stored in an employee's record will probably not be used to calculate pay but will be displayed on many personnel and labor reports. The package absolutely must allow user-defined fields to be accessed from the report writer.

Access to the Field from the Compute and Update Phases

Many packages allow operations on employee data during the update and compute phases. These operations may include moving data from one location to another or adding, subtracting, multiplying, or dividing two fields. Some systems even allow conditional execution of these operations to depend on the status of various fields. This provides a convenient way to implement benefit accrual programs. For example, if an employee is eligible for vacation, the company may wish to add 8 hours to their vacation accrual for each pay cycle worked.

External Dictionary Definition of the Field

Definitions should be made externally in a data dictionary because there will be many of them and they will change.

TRANSACTIONS AND THE PAYROLL CYCLE

Sequence of Transactions

Because of the complexity of payroll processing, most vendors code and sequence transactions so that several transactions can be entered for an employee in a single cycle. This eliminates confusion and makes the system easier to use. Thus it is usually possible to add an employee, input a handwritten check, input a void check, pay the employee for normal hours, pay the employee a bonus, and terminate him or her—all in one cycle.

In order to accommodate multiple transactions in one cycle, transactions are sequenced to take effect in a prescribed order. This affects the payroll processing. Unless the package can process transactions in the order a company wants, it becomes very awkward to submit transactions. One may have to set up a tickler file to submit some transactions in a future cycle. The normal sequence of transactions is the following:

1. Deletions.
2. Additions.
3. Changes and terminations.
4. Adjustments (void checks followed by handwritten checks).
5. Changes and terminations.
6. Time cards.
7. Additional checks and bonuses.
8. Changes and terminations.

Notice that changes and terminations can occur before adjustments, after adjustments, and after payment. This flexibility allows the natural sequence of entering a handwritten final check for a termination followed by a change of status before normal pay is calculated. Or an employee could be payed one last normal check and then be terminated—without someone having to remember to submit the termination in the following cycle. Similarly, one could change data that affect subsequent adjustments or time cards in the same pay cycle. Not all packages allow this freedom in entering transactions.

Adjustments, such as handwritten and voided checks, must be processed before normal pay because adjustments to taxable wages and withholdings are affected dramatically by the sequence, especially when employees approach the limits for these withholdings.

Tax Calculation

Most packages have parameter tables for the calculation of federal and state income taxes as well as local taxes. Never waste time on a package without this. Taxes change too frequently, and this is where most maintenance to payroll accounting occurs.

The vendors provide tax routines to handle the basic taxes. The routines calculate federal income tax (FIT), state income tax (SIT) for each of the states, social security tax for the Federal Industrial Compensation Act (FICA), and some of the major state disability insurance taxes (SDI). They also calculate wages subject to federal unemployment insurance (FUI) and state unemployment insurance (SUI).

The tax routines normally ignore the myriad of local tax calculations. They may address a few major metropolitan taxes but rarely go beyond a couple in each state. In order to accommodate all of these taxes (Pennsylvania alone has more than 1200), packages must allow the user to define additional taxes. These are identified by a tax jurisdiction code, with the tax rate stored in a table. Even if the company is not currently doing business in an area with local tax jurisdictions, it needs the capability. Decisions about acquisitions, mergers, and expansion are made without regard to the taxation routines available in a payroll system. Also, the shift from federal to local budgeting is encouraging many localities to introduce local income taxes. In short, there is no escape from local taxation.

The issues to consider when evaluating tax calculation routines are:

1. How are tax jurisdictions identified?
2. How are multiple jurisdictions handled?
3. How are the various parameters required for each jurisdiction specified?
4. How are the calculations defined for additional tax jurisdictions?
5. What happens when employees transfer from one tax jurisdiction to another?

Let us examine these individually.

How Are Tax Jurisdictions Identified?

Each state may be identified as a tax jurisdiction in a variety of ways. The most common tax routine uses the two-character postal abbreviation to identify a state. Thus California is "CA" and Iowa is "IA." Another tack taken in coding the jurisdictions is to use a numerical code for the state. One scheme numbers the states in alphabetical order. Thus Alabama is "01" and Wyoming is "50." Probably the worst coding system is one used by a vendor with one of the best tax calculation routines. Numeric codes are arbitrarily assigned to each state.

The state tax code may seem a minor detail, but the number of errors in tax calculation and reporting that occur because of the unwieldiness of the coding structure is amazing. A code of "OR" for Oregon and "CO" for Colorado is difficult to mistake, but in an arbitrary coding scheme the states might be "12" and "21."

How Are Multiple Tax Jurisdictions Handled?

Multiple tax jurisdictions present a very sticky problem. They cannot be avoided. Usually they occur when an employee lives in one state and works in another, but they may also occur with local tax jurisdictions. Local tax jurisdictions are worse because the jurisdictions involved may not agree on the solution. The major bordering states usually have an agreement and policy on reciprocity and multiple taxation.

In any case, the company will probably calculate taxes on prorated income for the jurisdictions affected. Make sure that the package can accommodate this.

How Are the Various Parameters Required for Each Jurisdiction Specified?

Unfortunately, the states differ on their methods of calculating taxes. It is not simply a matter of different tax brackets, but more a basic difference in the way exemptions are handled. Some states allow standard exemptions for both the marital status and the number of dependents. Other states concern themselves only with the number of dependents, and still others use only dollar amounts instead of dependents for various familial situations. One state even has two classes of dependents—those in the "family" and those classified as "other." Finally, one state ignores most of the issue and takes either 10 or 20% of federal income tax withholding, depending on the marital status.

To accommodate all of the state taxes using the traditional federal tax parameters of marital status and dependents requires some awkward "kluges." For example, the most popular tax calculation package treats the dependents field as two separate digits for some states. Thus a dependent code of "22" in one state means 22 dependents but in another means 2 "spouse" dependents (self and spouse) and 2 "other" dependents (children). This is necessary because some states allow a different exemption for children than they do for spouse.

Obviously, a coding structure dependent on the federal tax concept is confusing. Another major system uses an eight-character field to convey state tax parameters. Depending on the state, it may contain the marital status and number of dependents, an actual dollar amount exemption, or a percentage. This is a better solution than abusing the marital status and dependents field, but it still leaves something to be desired because it is difficult to generate a readable tax report since each state requires a different interpretation of the field.

Most of the tax calculation routines contain kluges as a result of wear or age. To handle multiple tax jurisdictions, a package could use the following items in the master file. Most packages do not have all of them.

Federal tax marital status

State tax marital status (Many packages do not allow a separate tax status for state; they use federal instead.)

Federal tax dependents

State tax dependents—Type A (spouse and self)

State tax dependents—Type B (children, parents)

State tax dependents—Type C (other)

State tax exemption dollar amount A

State tax exemption dollar amount B

How Are the Calculations Defined for Additional Tax Jurisdictions?

As mentioned, additional tax jurisdictions must be defined for the areas in which the company is doing business or in which it has employees. These definitions must be easy to implement and easy to change. This means that the package must have a table-driven tax routine. If a package requires that someone do programming to calculate these taxes, maintenance will be constant to keep up with the local taxes.

Several types of calculation are needed. They should include percentages of other taxes, such as a percentage of FIT or SIT, as well as the traditional percentage of gross and graduated income taxes. For graduated taxes, the package should be able to accept a table of entries with ranges of annual income. Each range should carry a fixed dollar amount corresponding to the taxes of all income up to the beginning of the range, as well as a percentage to be applied to the employee's income which exceeds the minimum for the range. This is the standard definition for graduated income and is used for FIT and most SIT calculations.

Many local tax calculations have a limit. These calculations require the same basic features that FICA does. That is, they are usually based on a subset of earnings. For example, a state disability tax may be applied against all earnings except sick pay and disability pay, subject to a limit. Thus employees would not pay more than a certain amount for a calendar year.

To properly calculate taxes that are subject to a limit, a package needs two features: it should stop withholding tax as soon as the limit is reached; and it should recalculate the tax each cycle with the total liability (including previously taxed wages). Once the total tax is calculated against the total liability, the tax can be compared with what has been withheld to determine how much need be withheld or refunded in the current cycle.

What Happens when Employees Transfer from One Tax Jurisdiction to Another?

The same problem occurs in transferring from one corporate entity to another. Tax transfers are a sticky issue for most payrolls. When an employee transfers from one tax jurisdiction to another, the information from the previous jurisdiction must be saved and room made for accumulations in the new jurisdiction. Taxable wages and tax withholdings cannot be lumped together because they must be reported separately on W-2 and 941A forms.

Transfers become even more complicated when an employee who has transferred then transfers back to the original jurisdiction. If this occurs, it is not enough to store the current jurisdiction and make room for a new one. Accumulations for the original tax jurisdiction must be retrieved, and the new taxes must begin adding to these. This complicated process absolutely dictates that tax location changes be processed specially. It is not the same as a change of department or last name. There must also be adequate room on the employee record for the number of transfers that can occur in a calendar year.

Often the tax transfer occurs in a transfer from one division or subsidiary to another. This further complicates the process because it may require that SUI, FUI, or FICA accumulations be set to zero, depending on the federal and state tax IDs in use in the two locations.

Tax calculations must be correct. It is true that tax withholdings are made on behalf of the employee, and the employer has no control over whether the employee ultimately files a tax return. There have been, however, a number of recent court decisions that have increased the liability of the employer for correctly withholding taxes.

In certain instances where the employer failed to withhold for multiple states or where the employee was allowed to claim 99 exemptions to avoid withholdings, the taxing authority was able to place responsibility on the employer and collect taxes that should have been withheld. This implies that a company should correctly withhold taxes and be careful in securing proper documents and waivers from employees when establishing dependents and exemptions.

PUSH DOWN STACKS AND PERSONNEL INFORMATION

One of the significant data collection tasks in a personnel system is history. A company wants a history of salary increases, job changes, organizational transfers, reviews, and many other things as well. These data constitute a "stack" or list of information, that grows with time but also varies in length from employee to employee. That is, while each employee will have only one social security number, one employee may have a 10-year history of semiannual raises while another may be a recent hire with no raise or review yet.

From a data processing perspective, storing these lists is much more complicated than simply making room for a piece of data and storing it. As each addition to the stack of information is made, the next available location must be found and the data stored in it. On one employee's record, the next location may be the third spot in the stack while for a different employee it may be the sixth.

One must also resolve what to do when the stack is full. In some cases the oldest entry is deleted. This would occur if a history of the last 10 absences were to be saved. In other situations, the oldest element is retained and the second to oldest deleted. This is used for salary history so that the original salary is always saved. When a history of income or hours worked is being accumulated, the deleted items are rolled up or added to the last element. In other words, if a stack of hours worked has room for 10 years of history, the last element in the stack might be used to accumulate prior years when the stack becomes full.

The ability to maintain stacks is a must for a personnel/payroll system. Fortunately, most packages have this feature. More than this, however, several features are needed in the stacks.

1. One should be able to designate fields that will be stored in the stack. The fields should include any user-defined fields that are desired.
2. One should be able to designate "triggers" for a stack that will cause history to be saved. In other words, if a trigger field changes, such as salary, then an element should be stored in the stack.
3. One should be able to define more than one stack for each employee record.
4. One should be able to designate more than one "trigger" for a stack, such as both salary and job classification.
5. One should be able to control the number of items in a stack.
6. One should be able to control what happens to the last element in a stack when it becomes full. The normal options are to delete it, delete the next to last, or add up numeric totals.

HIGH-VOLUME CHANGES

Most systems offer high-volume change transactions. This is not a must, but it is convenient. This feature allows the user to input one generic transaction that will be applied to every employee. For example, suppose at the beginning of each quarter someone wishes to zero out the sick hours taken field on every employee's record. Rather than submitting transactions for each employee, a single high-volume transaction can be submitted to zero the field for every employee.

Rarely does one want to change a single field to a single value for every employee. More often, the change is made only for a certain subset of employees. Or the field may be changed by incrementing or decrementing it by a percentage, as for across-the-board increases. To do this, the mass change capability needs to have some conditions tied to it that restrict its application to only employees meeting the right criteria.

Most across-the-board or without-exception situations turn out in fact to be "across the board . . . except for employees in department 512, members of Union Local 718 and anyone born on Tuesday. . . . " Even if the mass change feature is blessed with the ability to restrict it to certain conditions, it is unlikely that a single mass transaction will accomplish the goal.

The mass change transaction is itself something of a loaded gun, and in the wrong hands, it is literally dangerous. It may be easier, safer, and more appropriate to take another tack in generating transactions. Most of personnel/payroll packages have report writers that can generate transaction images (records in the image of input transactions). Thus the report writer can be used to read the existing master file and generate transactions for employees meeting the correct criteria. This gives several advantages. First, data processing will normally become involved, and this helps provide a check against the incorrect or unnecessary use of a very powerful and dangerous tool. Second, the criteria and logic decisions available through the report writer are more sophisticated than those available with the mass change feature. Finally, a supporting report can be generated and the transactions double-checked before they are input.

As an opinion, the mass change or high-volume transaction is convenient in a few cases but overrated in most.

TRANSACTION GENERATORS

At least two major packages offer the ability to test employee records for certain conditions and generate transactions if needed. This is different from using the report writer or the mass change feature described above because it is an integral part of the payroll cycle and is usually based on information embedded in the employee's record.

Generated transactions typically take effect only one time for each employee, and they usually are controlled by date to occur at strategic points in each employee's life at the company. An example is turning on benefits such as medical, life, and dental plans, pension eligibility, and tenure. Each of these might be controlled by the length of employment. A change generator is particularly convenient for step pay increases. If a company has employees in bargaining units who are guaranteed step increases after some time period, a transaction generator is an ideal way to implement the changes. It is easiest to think of a transaction generator as a built-in tickler file of transactions that are released into the system at strategic points. However, the more powerful generators are capable of inspecting a series of conditions to cause the generation of a particular transaction. In this way, the conditions can be specified for the entire file rather than being specified for each employee.

LABOR DISTRIBUTION AND GENERAL LEDGER INTERFACES

A payroll system collects detailed information that can drive labor and project accounting systems and provide information for journal vouchers to a general ledger system. All labor costs funnel through a payroll system. In addition to costs, time can be funneled through the system too. By the same token, direct salary expenses can be summarized and routed to general ledger, along with employer expenses (FUI, SUI, FICA), the liability for tax withholdings, and voluntary deductions.

Most packages generate transaction files for labor distribution and general ledger. These transaction files can be fed into other systems. Although the file may need to be summarized and reformatted for the general ledger, it should contain the necessary data at the necessary level of detail. Look for the following items:

1. All labor costs, including normal pay, adjustments, and bonuses, must be funneled out of payroll into labor distribution/general ledger.

2. All earnings should remain at the lowest level of detail coming out of payroll, and the summarization should be done later. This gives the opportunity to segregate various earnings types (regular, overtime, vacation, holiday, and sick) and post them to separate salary expense accounts as necessary.

3. All deductions should be funneled through as well. Labor distribution will not be concerned with them, with the possible exception of FICA. However, they represent an employer liability that must be reported to general ledger.

4. FICA, SUI, and FUI wages should be sent on to general ledger to facilitate the calculation of employer expenses for these figures.

5. There should be a way to pass additional data elements along to labor distribution and general ledger to facilitate special calculations or reporting that is done in these areas. Examples include the employee home department, shift, job classification, base rate, and tax location.

General ledger data usually are easy to interface. It is simply a matter of summarizing expenses to the level of detail required by the chart of accounts and organizational structure and formatting the results into journal voucher transactions. However, if the payroll cycle does not match the accounting cycle, then pay must be accrued to the proper accounting periods. This frequently occurs when the pay period is two weeks and the accounting period four weeks. The accrual is best done in the interface itself without complicating the payroll process.

The labor distribution interface is a bit more complicated. Most packages offer some type of labor reporting, but a quick review makes one wonder why they bother. In practice, these features are rarely used. Instead, a labor cost file is used to drive a home-grown labor distribution system or possibly a packaged project accounting system.

To drive a labor or project accounting system, the payroll system must output a labor cost file with enough detail to include a labor distribution code (as input on the time card), each detail earnings type, the shift the employee worked, as well as hours by category. This implies that any one employee may have more than one record, depending on how the employee's time is charged and what shifts he or she work.

There is a problem allocating employer expenses for FICA, FUI, and SUI. Typically, packages compute the employer's FICA, FUI, and SUI based on the employee's earnings, but they do not spread them across the labor distribution codes in which the employees worked. If a company charges these expenses to overhead, there is no problem. However, if the company charges these items as direct expenses to the centers in which the employees worked, a fairly sophisticated allocation is necessary.

PERSONNEL REPORTING

While most payroll functions are accounting tasks, personnel functions are generally reporting tasks. There are two basic types of personnel reports, those external to the company and those internal to the company.

Government-Mandated Reports

The federal government exerts a constant demand for reports from the personnel departments of most large companies. The decade of the 1970s heralded the birth of a whole alphabet of personnel reports—EEO, ERISA, OSHA, and on and on. These reports are all mandated by the federal government and its agencies.

Unfortunately, these reports constantly change. They changed while this book was being written. They are likely to change again as you read this paragraph and probably once again before you finish this chapter.

Other Outside Agency Reporting

Many companies must prepare and submit statistical information to other agencies and institutions outside the company. For example, large aerospace and defense contractors often submit statistical information about professional and nonprofessional employee compensation to institutions that collect these data to provide industrial standards. This information is both voluminous and detailed, and is best provided by an automated system. Even the labor unions are getting into the act and demanding information from companies prior to bargaining.

Internal Reporting

Benefits have become an increasing part of employee compensation. This has drastically increased the need for personnel reports. There is a whole series of reports likely to be needed by any large company. The benefits reports may include anniversary lists, benefit status reports, medical and life insurance listings, HMO eligibility lists, salary history reports, and many more. Besides the increase in reporting related to benefits, there has also been a strong push toward recording skills inventory data for each employee. The information collected includes college education, languages spoken, and technical skills.

How Do the Package Systems Cope?

Faced with this confusing array of personnel reporting requirements, package systems have difficulty responding. Some packages have attempted to stay on top of all governmental requirements and provide specific reporting modules to answer each need. Such vendors have a difficult time keeping up.

Other vendors have recognized that they cannot hope to keep up with the reporting needs. They have taken a longer view by developing systems that facilitate collecting a mass of personnel data through the use of user-defined fields described earlier in this chapter. The idea is that if a company can store the information it needs, it is then relatively easy to dredge it up later with a report writer.

It is important to note, however, that personnel reporting does not just require storing reams of information about current employees. The EEO reports require data about applicants (who may never have been hired) as well as terminated employees.

ERISA (Employee Retirement Income Security Act) has a very confusing set of vesting requirements that suggest that a company should retain information about terminated employees for at least as long as they were employed. In other words, if someone was employed for nine years and then terminated, the company should keep their retirement vesting information for at least another nine years.

In general, if a company is looking for a system that will solve its personnel reporting requirements, it should look for the following:

1. The system should have some convenient means for retaining inactive employees. There will be many individuals that it wishes to retain on file, without putting them through the normal payroll cycle.

2. The system should have some means of tracking applicants separately from employees.

3. The system should offer user-defined data areas for adding future information requirements.

4. The system should have a report writer that is flexible enough to generate both listings, such as anniversary and benefit status reports, and matrix-type reports like the EEO series.

Chapter 10
General Ledger
Packages

General ledger packages are more than just automated general ledgers. They are generalized financial control systems that not only post detail transactions but also summarize the data into financial statements and balance sheets. In addition, many general ledger packages do allocations, consolidations, and budgeting.

With general ledger packages, the basic concept is to post detail transactions against a chart of accounts. The chart of accounts is the company's list of authorized account numbers.

Because accounting information often is reported by account, organization, and project, the posting is done to this level of detail. Each individual detail line item is posted to three numbers (a three-tuple): account number, organization (corporation, division, department, etc.), and project (task or job code).

This three-tuple structure is used to generate a variety of reports. Data can be summarized by account for balance sheet reports, profit and loss statements, and other traditional accounting reports. By selecting and summarizing data by organization, departmental cost analyses and profit center performance reports are produced. Project accounting reports, product reports, and job accounting reports are produced by selecting and summarizing data by project.

A package needs this three-tuple architecture for posting. Even if a company does not currently require reporting by organizational unit or project, it will sooner or later. (More likely, immediately after the package is implemented.) The ability to post to a three-tuple is such an integral part of a package design that it cannot be added to one that does not have it. Nothing is impossible, but adding a three-tuple structure to a package that does not have it comes close.

Each of the items in the three-tuple may be a hierarchy. This is most obvious for the organizational portion of the three-tuple. Every company has a hierarchy for reporting, starting at the corporate level and moving down through subsidiaries, divisions, plants, departments, and groups.

Most charts of accounts also have a hierarchy embedded within them. Thus current assets may be one account that includes several narrower areas of accounts, including cash and accounts receivable. These in turn may be broken down into more detailed accounts. Thus cash may consist of cash in banks, cash on deposit, and credit lines. Even these more detailed accounts may represent summarizations of specific detail accounts, such as cash in particular bank accounts. Some companies use a prime account/subaccount scheme for the account hierarchy. Thus cash in banks may be account 1001 while cash in bank account 10234 is 1001.01 and cash in account 45678 is 1001.02. The important thing is not the numbering scheme but that a hierarchy exists.

Project reporting usually has a structure of its own, too. A series of detail tasks may constitute a single project, which, when lumped with other projects, represents a master project.

The implementation of hierarchical structures is critical to the ease of use and efficient performance of any general ledger package. There are two popular ways of providing hierarchical information, which are described in the following sections. They are the "detail" and "data base" methods. They differ in the way that detail is posted and maintained in files. Neither approach is superior. Both can be good or bad, depending on the needs.

DETAIL APPROACH

The detail approach to maintaining general ledger information is like the old, manual method of posting transactions to subsidiary ledgers. Transactions are accumulated in detailed files and posted in chronological order. Picture the accounting clerk sitting at a high desk writing individual journal entries onto a magnetic tape with a magnetic pen instead of posting them in an old musty ledger.

In the manual environment, when it came time to produce balance sheets and income statements, it was a lot of work. Individual ledgers were summarized to produce totals for the reports. Reporting with the automated detail approach is done much the same way, except the computer does the work. To produce reports, the detail files are read and data are selected, sorted, and summarized for reporting. This selection and sorting can be extensive, depending on the reporting done.

Most packages adopting the detail approach create periodic summary files to minimize the run cost. These summary files accumulate detail transactions into abbreviated files for reporting. Several levels of summary files may be created for different types of report. These levels are similar to the levels of totals on a traditional report: subtotals, totals, and grand totals.

Here is an example. Suppose a detail transactions file is subtotaled by account number, organization code, and project number. There would be a file of subtotals for each unique three-tuple used for posting. This file would be much smaller than the detail file, especially if many transactions were posted. This file could be used to produce any reports that did not require the detail. It could easily produce a report that lists expenses by department or one that shows income by project.

Let us take the example a step further. If the summary file is next summarized by account number alone, the result is a smaller file: a level-two summary, so to speak. This file has only one record for each unique account number. The file lacks the detail necessary to produce department or project reports, but it can produce balance sheets, income statements, and any other accounting reports that depend on account number.

This example is simplified, but the point remains that there is considerable savings in time and machine resources with summary files. The data base approach takes this a step further. Since it is obvious that the summarized information often is used in reports, why not make this summarization a part of the posting process? This is the basis of the data base approach.

DATA BASE APPROACH

With the data base approach, transactions are accumulated into fields or buckets in a data base. This data base is similar to post office boxes. In the data base approach, each unique three-tuple combination of numbers gets a separate bucket. Now, picture an accounting clerk sorting and accumulating transactions into the individual buckets. This is how the data base approach works.

To produce reports, the report writer need only print the buckets that contain the data of interest, in the same way that people can locate their mail without having to look through all the other post office boxes.

Again, the example is greatly simplified. Each bucket described here may consist of many buckets. A single account three-tuple may have buckets for current period, prior periods, year periods (one package goes back five years), and even budgets. Moreover, many packages using the data base approach have separate account buckets for automatic roll-ups or summaries. Packages with this feature automatically post summary accounts, such as current assets, whenever a detail account, such as cash in bank, is posted.

Similarly, summary three-tuples may be kept to summarize by organization and project hierarchies. If an amount is posted to a department, the amount can be automatically rolled up the organizational hierarchy to the division, subsidiary, and company levels. Since these accumulations are done automatically during posting, much of the work of reporting is finished before reporting begins.

It sounds great. There are, however, a number of drawbacks to this approach. Let us compare the advantages and disadvantages of the two approaches.

Defining the Accounting Structure

With the detail approach, only the detail account three-tuples that are used need to be defined. The hierarchy can be defined on an ad hoc basis when reports are created. Because the detail is always available, the hierarchy and the summarization can be changed at any time. Does the CFO want to split a division or consolidate 11 departments? No problem; it can be done.

On the other hand, a data base requires that all of the buckets be created before posting. The hierarchy buckets are defined at the same time. This is inherently inflexible. If the organization is restructured, the data base must be restructured as well. The existing hierarchies and summaries are no longer valid with the new structure. The vendors do offer so-called high-volume transactions for this kind of maintenance, but it is still a lot of work. In fact, the effort to establish the data base becomes a large part of the installation of the package.

Use of Machine Resources

There is a big difference in the use of hardware devices with the two approaches. The detail approach is essentially sequential, and so tapes can be freely substituted for disks. With the data base approach, however, there must be sufficient disk space for the entire data base. Consider again the post office analogy. If all New Yorkers were to have their own post office boxes, the result would be a very large building.

If a company has a complex chart of accounts or if it is supporting multiple charts of accounts, the disk requirements may be extensive— even overwhelming.

Reporting

The data base approach has the advantage over the detail approach for reporting. Both approaches can produce the same reports, but it is easier and faster with the data base approach.

In summary, it is difficult to set down hard and fast rules for selecting one approach over the other. However, as a rule of thumb, larger, more complex charts of accounts with fewer detail transactions are better served by the detail approach. Smaller, more rigid hierarchical charts with high volumes of detail transactions favor the data base approach.

What does a company do if it has a large, complex chart of accounts and a high volume of detail transactions? The best approach is to try to locate other companies that face the same problem. If an industry dictates the complexity of the chart of accounts, then the company's competitors are probably in the same boat. Find out how they cope. At the very least, there is someone else with whom to drown one's sorrows.

SPECIFIC GENERAL LEDGER FUNCTIONS

Regardless of the approach, there are several other considerations in selecting general ledger packages. These include budgeting, reporting, posting, closing, automatic entries, memo entries, and allocations. Although allocations are listed last, they are one of the most complex aspects of general ledger.

Budgeting

Most packages offer budgeting, either integrated into the package or as an add-on module. Buy it, by all means.

Budgets are handled in several ways. The budgets may be stored right with the account data or they may be kept in a separate file. The important thing is that the package allows budgeting at the level of detail needed, and that the budgets can be accessed with the report writer. For example, can budgets be specified by period or must a yearly budget be specified and then allocated? Often there is a need to do both. With a package using the data base approach, can budgeting be done at any level in the hierarchy or must it be done at the detail level only? What happens if budgeting is done at both the detail and summary levels? Can budgets be changed once they are input? Will the package keep track of the original budget as well as the revised budget? What happens if yet a third revision is made? Can the package create a forecasted budget based on actual amounts posted? If so, how does it do it?

Many companies use variable budgets and the package vendors have responded. Variable budgets include both a fixed and a variable amount. The fixed amount represents costs or incomes that do not vary with activity. Rent, insurance, and overhead are likely candidates. Variable budget amounts are not amounts, but rather formulas that compute amounts for a period. Usually the formula is a simple percentage of another figure, such as gross sales or salaries. Some packages allow the formula to be based on any quantity that is posted in the general ledger. For example, the formula may depend on units produced, patients treated, units sold, or square footage.

A company must consider its own budgeting needs carefully when evaluating a budgeting feature. Are variable budgets needed? What are the formulas? Try expressing a few of these with the vendors method. Do they work?

Chart of Accounts

For a data base approach, the chart of accounts constitutes the data base, and so there is no problem in supporting separate charts of accounts for separate entities. Each entity's accounts represent unique tuples because the entity number is part of the three-tuple.

With the detail approach, the chart of accounts is handled differently. A table file lists all the valid accounts, gives their descriptions, and includes their attributes. Make sure that this file contains an organization or corporate code to accompany the account number. Otherwise the company may be stuck with a package that supports only one chart of accounts. Vendors sometimes say that a package can be run with different input files to support multiple charts. Anyone who thinks that this will not be a logistic nightmare will be interested in some prime swamp land that the authors are unloading.

Attributes for accounts should not be predefined in a package. A company must also be able to define and update its own accounts. They should not be preprogrammed or hard-wired into the package.

Likewise, the package must not restrict the assignment of accounts to arbitrary ranges of numbers. For example, a package might restrict assets to accounts numbered between 10000 and 19999. A company may not want this.

Reporting

The packages provide report writers rather than canned reports because every company's accounting reports are different. These report writers are matrix oriented. They can produce summaries in which specific account three-tuples are rolled up and printed on specific lines on a page. Chapter 15 contains a more complete discussion of report writers.

Report definitions should be maintained separately and not incorporated into the master file or data base. In other words, if one wishes to create a new report it would be nice if new input to the report writer were the only requirement. Some implementations don't allow this.

One major package requires that maintenance be performed on the data base itself to define a report. To include a particular account three-tuple on a specific report line, one must update that account three-tuple to point to the proper report number and line number. This means that some poor soul must do maintenance on every account that is to appear on the report. The master file then carries all this excess report baggage around with it. Changes are very difficult to make. Even with high-volume maintenance features that allow generic account changes, there is a lot of work involved. This is particularly aggravating because the report will be wrong the first few times it is tested, which requires yet more maintenance. This is not a major problem if the reports seldom change, but it certainly discourages ad hoc reporting.

The report writer should be able to summarize three-tuples onto specific lines, with columns representing various periods, accumulations of periods, or budgets. In addition, there should be a way to include descriptions for each line.

One should be able to define a line with a report writer in terms of other lines. For example, line 15 may be current assets, which is the total of lines 2 through 13. Line 21 may be long-term assets, the total of lines 17–19. If line 23 is total assets, it is the sum of lines 15 and 21. Expressing lines in terms of other lines is much more flexible and efficient than defining each line in terms of the account tuples that summarize into it.

The report writer should be able to express columns in terms of each other. For example, column C may be the difference between column A (actual current period) and column B (budget current period). Some packages provide rather sophisticated columnar arithmetic, with percentages, multiplication, and other formulas. This makes it easy to generate a forecast column based on cost or income history.

The report format is also an important consideration. Can the column size and spacing be changed? Can amounts in columns be scaled to dollars and cents, dollars only, or dollars in thousands? Can lines with only zeroes in them be suppressed? How does the report writer handle division by zero? Does it assume a value of zero and go on, or does it abnormally terminate the program? What happens to any other figures that depend on the results of this computation, such as column and row totals?

A few vendors supply a detail report writer along with a matrix report writer. Chapter 15 describes detail report writers. They are useful for audit reports that list and summarize detail transactions. They are a valuable tool for analysis of particular accounts.

Far more common than detail report writers are graphics packages. These display financial data graphically rather than as printed lines. They can produce bar graphs, line graphs, and even pie charts. The graphics packages can print graphs on the standard impact, thermal, and laser printers. The graphs have low resolution and are not all that aesthetic. Low-resolution pictures come out like attempts to draw the Mona Lisa on a typewriter. The more sophisticated graphics packages can draw graphs on graphic devices, often with color. These graphs have high resolution and are of high quality. It is a good idea to have a heavy technical person, such as a systems programmer, evaluate any graphics package to be sure that the company has the required graphics hardware.

Posting

Transactions are usually edited in batches and validated against the chart of accounts before being posted. This control is essential. Batch controls should be on both debits and credits. A hash total across all of the account numbers provides even more control.

Besides batch controls, the package edits the individual transactions as well. The package should validate the account, the organization, and the project, as well as combinations of these. This is inherent in the data base approach, but it may not be provided in a detail system.

Look closely at how the package handles invalid transactions. If the handling is inconvenient, it will cause a real nightmare. Because of the time it takes to collect and process all of the data that feed general ledger, the closing schedule is very tight. If large batches of data are being posted, the company may not want the package to reject an entire batch just because an individual account is incorrect. It may want the package to post the incorrect account to a suspense account. This lets the books be closed and reports produced. Later, someone can worry about resolving the suspended amount.

Do not assume that the suspense accounting feature just described exists in a package just because the package is complex and sophisticated. One of the more popular and sophisticated packages does not provide this feature.

Closing

The term "closing" means the ending of one accounting period and the beginning of another. It is difficult to be much more specific because there are as many methods of closing as there are packages. The method of closing depends entirely on the structure and organization of the data.

Closing is a barrier placed between one cycle and another. Once the books are closed for the current period, all current period figures become prior period figures. The new prior period figures are no longer affected by standard journal voucher transactions because the books are technically closed. Some packages do allow prior period adjustments that affect historical data.

In packages based on the detail approach, closing means creating summary files for reports, and archiving the current period detail onto magnetic tape or computer output microfiche (COM).

For packages using the data base approach, closing may require just moving the current period buckets to prior period slots. Depending on the structure of the data base, the closing may be accomplished by changing file pointers to point to new buckets in the data base.

The most important thing about closing is the time it takes. The closing cycle may have a window of only a few hours. People like the CFO begin breathing fire if the closing schedule is not met. Closing the system in one company was so difficult that it took 22 hours. Unfortunately, the schedule allowed only 24 hours—no room for mistakes. Even if a company has ample time for closing, it may not have time to do it twice. Inevitably a month will come along when the payroll transactions are incorrect and no one catches it until after closing. There must be time to correct mistakes.

Automatic Entries

Many packages can post selected entries automatically. This eliminates drudgery and also reduces the chance for errors. There are several different types of automatic entry. The vendors have even trademarked some of the names.

One type, the recurring journal entry, automatically generates a new entry with the same amount each period. Thus a single entry can be made for rental expense, and it will be posted automatically until someone request it to stop. It is even better if a start and stop date can be set on the original transaction. This ensures that the transactions are posted correctly without the worry that someone will forget to turn them off.

A second type of automatic entry is one that provides the offsetting entry for a single transaction. This could be used to provide the offsetting entry of accumulated depreciation to offset depreciation expense. A third type of entry automatically generates a reversing transaction, often in a later accounting period. This is used for entering estimated costs, such as quarterly taxes, into a system, and then automatically reversing them at quarter end when the actual figures are available.

There are several considerations with automatic entries. First, do they really save enough time and effort to justify their use? If they are important to a company, then one should carefully review what they do and how they are used. Two packages, both offering recurring journal entries, may differ dramatically in power and ease of use. There is no such thing as a standard automatic entry.

Memo Entries

Some packages allow memo or statistical entries to be posted to the general ledger. Statistics and other numeric data about the business can be gathered, right along with the dollar activity. This feature is particularly useful for performance reporting. Cost, income (or profit per unit), and variable budgeting by unit are examples. As described later, statistics also can be used for allocation.

Currency Conversion

The international aspect of modern businesses often makes it necessary to convert currency and express balance sheets and income statements in terms of other currencies. This leads to a number of unique problems, not the least of which is the conversion itself. There are problems in scale, in the conversion timing, and in formatting results for printing.

The conversion itself is usually performed via a table of exchange rates that a user sets up. However, conversion rates change daily. Historical information may require that a table contain more than one rate of exchange.

The way the amount actually is stored in a file is also important. Packages usually want the amounts to be stored in dollars. They are then converted to other currencies as necessary. This is all right for capital assets other than cash and accounts receivable. But cash in foreign banks does not vary with exchange rates. For this, the currency should be stored in the native form: dollars, lira, pounds, and so on.

Unfortunately, this leads to scaling problems. Suppose that a package is designed to handle amounts as large as a billion dollars. A billion dollars becomes a number in the trillions when converted to yen or lira. This causes problems in fitting the columns onto a page in reports, but even worse, the data may not fit in the fields of the file.

A minor problem is that the use of commas and a period in numbers is not an international standard. In Europe, their roles are reversed. We in the United States would write a number as:

$$11,375.65$$

In West Germany it is written as:

$$11.375,65$$

IBM and most other computer vendors recognize this problem and provide for it in their programming languages. However, this same foresight may not be present in packages for financial applications.

Many companies choose not to implement their general ledger and financial systems abroad. They prefer to allow the managers in those locations to develop their own financial reporting consistent with accepted business practices in the countries in which they operate. This is fine, but it makes comparison reporting and consolidations difficult. A company may choose not to force a package on its foreign subsidiaries, but it is still a good idea to implement foreign currencies to ease consolidation and to provide domestic executives with standard basis of information.

Allocations

Allocations are the most complicated part of implementing a general ledger system. Because of the many ways allocations are done, it is difficult to provide general solutions. The methods include base/pool allocations, percentage allocations, fixed allocations, and stepdown allocations, to name but a few. All are similar in concept but vastly different in operation.

The basic concept of allocation is to collect a pool of amounts that represent income or expenses and allocate or spread these amounts based on some formula or methodology. Let us consider the example of overhead expenses that are to be allocated to profit centers.

Overhead expenses are usually charged en masse against overhead or indirect centers within a company. No immediate attempt is made to charge utility bills, rent, and administrative salaries back to the centers that benefited from them. It is too difficult to measure the gas, electricity, and water used by each department within a company unless the department has its own metering. It is even more difficult to measure the amount of executive and management labor expended on each department within a company.

Instead of trying to charge the departments directly, the costs are allocated. A simple allocation may spread the overhead expenses evenly among several departments. More commonly, a percentage distribution is used. Department A may get 10% of the overhead, department B 35%, and department C 55%. The percentages usually are established by management and adjusted periodically. The percentages often are tied to performance criteria. For example, the allocation might be based on a percentage of the employees or floor space. If the basis is something more volatile, such as units produced, salary expense, costs, or sales, it would be nice to have the package automatically recalculate the percentages each period. This is the basis of base/pool allocations.

Packages that offer base/pool allocations allow the user to identify a base of accounts that is to share a pool of accumulated expenses or income. Along with specifying the base, the user identifies a basis, which can be an account or a method that is used to calculate a percentage share for each department in the base. Thus the user could identify departments A, B, and C as the base, salary expense as the basis, and fringe benefits as the pool to allocate. The package determines each department's share of the pool by using each department's share of the base to prorate the pool.

If A has salaries of $15,000, B has $10,000, and C has $25,000, the total base is $50,000. Department A has a 30% share of this base, B has 20%, and C has 50%. If the pool of fringe benefits is $25,000, A gets $7500, B gets $5000, and C gets $12,500. This may appear identical to the percentage method described above. It is. The difference is that the package calculates the percentages instead of having them input. If the salary expenses change in the next period, the percentages will vary accordingly.

Some companies complicate the allocation problem by having several iterations or layers of allocations. These are step-down allocations that occur in a series of steps or iterations. The process is as follows. One round of allocation is performed as described above. The result of this round then becomes a pool for another round of allocation. The process can be repeated as often as patience and computer time permit.

The better packages have separate allocations modules that can do all of the methods described above. Some packages do their allocations by using the report writer. This is a flexible approach, but it tends to be very time-consuming, especially with stepdown allocations.

Chapter 11
Accounts Receivable
Packages

Accounts receivable packages record and track the money owed by customers. The packages do not usually bill customers but rather accept invoices, payments, and adjustments in order to generate statements, aged trial balance reports, and general ledger transactions.

There are two distinct approaches to accounts receivable. These approaches differ in the way detail is maintained in files and in the way payments are applied. These approaches—balance forward and open item—predate automated systems.

BALANCE FORWARD ACCOUNTING

As consumers, we are all familiar with balance forward accounting. Department store charge cards, bank cards, medical bills, and utility bills all use balance forward accounting. To understand what this means, look at any statement for these items. There is a balance forward amount (always, it seems), along with the detail history of the current month's activity.

The current month's activity includes all charges, payments, and credits. However, there is no supporting detail history for the balance forward figure; it is merely a summarized amount. The detail history supporting the balance forward amount was printed in prior statements. The bottom of the statement contains the total amount owed, which is the total of the month's activity (the net effect of charges and payments) and the balance forward. This figure is the new balance and will appear next month as the balance forward. Cash and credits are applied to the outstanding balance rather than to particular items that have been charged.

Balance forward processing is convenient for consumer credit, especially revolving charge accounts. It has the major advantage of continually compressing the detail into a balance forward. This permits the high volume of detail charges in retail credit applications. Also, the clerks who apply cash payments need not be concerned with which items are actually being paid off. Imagine the difficulty an accounting clerk would have in trying to apply a department store payment to each item that a customer purchased:

"Let's see here, we have a $50.00 payment on the Jones account. That's $23.00 for the toaster and $18.95 for the towels. What should I do with this other $8.05? Partial payment on the sheets or on the candlesticks?"

Balance forward accounting has a couple of drawbacks. First, because the detail is summarized periodically, the accounts cannot be aged correctly. As a result, retail credit aging is based on the date of receipt of the last payment. Second, there is no itemization of what has been paid and what has not. When an invoice is sent out and a payment received, there is no way to tell if the amount was derived from the invoice.

If anyone has ever had the frustrating experience of having an incorrect charge applied to a retail credit account, the virtue of seeing payments and charges tied together in retail credit accounting is immediately clear.

The other approach to accounts receivable, open items processing, solves the problem of tying payments to individual items.

OPEN ITEMS ACCOUNTING

Most commercial accounts receivable are handled on an open items basis. Again, many people deal with these as consumers. A mortgage payment or installment credit payment is the best example.

When a cash payment is sent in for a loan, the payment is applied against a specific installment due. If too much is sent, the payment coupon requests that the sender tell where additional cash is to be applied. It can be applied to the balance of the loan or as a future payment. If the payment is too small, it is either applied as a partial payment against the installment or it is rejected. The balance of the installment is retained on file as a separate item that still remains to be paid.

Commercial accounts receivable are similar to installment accounting. Items are billed on invoices and the items are retained on file as open items until they are paid. As cash is received, the payments are applied against specific items on file. Once an item is paid in full, it is closed and can be purged. The current balance due is the sum of the balance due on the open items.

Open item processing provides several advantages. First, history is retained until items are paid off. Thus any statement generated carries the detail of all outstanding items. Second, cash is applied against specific invoices (which is the way commercial customers want to pay their accounts—by invoice). Third, because the accounts are maintained by item, it is easy to generate a complete aging of the account. It is also easy to determine how old any single item is in order to age the balance due on it.

Open item processing is not a panacea. Cash application is difficult because payments are applied against specific items. This is not as simple as balance forward cash applications, as we saw when the accounting clerk tried to spread a $50.00 payment.

Commercial customers usually identify the disbursement of their check on a remittance advice included with the payment. The remittance advice makes it a simple matter to post payment against specific items. However, customers are under no obligation to provide a remittance advice. Many do not. What then? Cash cannot just be applied to the account. Someone must identify the outstanding items and then decide how to apply the payment.

The sheer volume of charges presents a problem to an open item system. A balance forward system cleanses itself of detail each month. Open items detail clears only when it is paid off. There is almost twice as much detail in an open item system because payments are not applied to the outstanding balance but against specific items. One check payment may result in 12 payment transactions.

Neither the open item nor balance forward approach is inherently better. If there is a high volume of charges per customer, as in retail applications with revolving accounts, then balance forward is best. If the company does commercial accounts receivable, the open item method must be used.

What if a company needs both approaches? Large companies often need both balance forward and open item processing. One solution is to have two separate systems. Another is to use an open item system as a balance forward system.

An open item system can be made to function as a balance forward system. It will not perform as efficiently, but it can be done. To do it, statements are generated that summarize all the prior month's open items into a balance forward. From the customer's point of view, the statement looks like a balance forward statement.

Except for the cash receipts clerks, no one is the wiser. There is a problem in trying to apply cash payments to specific items. This is remedied by developing a cash application system that automatically applies and spreads cash against the oldest items on file.

This solution is best for those companies that require both approaches. It should not be used as a substitute for a balance forward system. Buy a balance forward system if that is all that is needed. Otherwise, the system is like a small car trying to pull a large trailer.

FILE STRUCTURE

An accounts receivable system contains data that may belong in several logically separate files. Depending on the package, the data may be combined in one physical file or stored in separate files. The data are logically distinct, however, so they will be treated that way here.

Customer Master File

This file contains all of the demographic data about the customer or client and may include some history as well. The file provides the addresses and names necessary to generate statements and other reports. The file should include at least the following elements:

Account number
Customer name
Customer address
Sales territory
Customer classification
High balance
Year to date purchases
Inception to date purchases
Dunn and Bradstreet code
Standard industrial code (SIC)
Customer bank account number
Customer sales contact
Sales contact telephone number
Customer accounts payable contact
Accounts payable contact telephone number
Accounts receivable cycle code

Some companies carry their own employees on file as customers. The employees may not actually be customers of the company, but they are treated this way for such employee receivable items as loans, copy machines, telephone service, stationery, and travel advances. If employees are carried in the files as customers, then at least the following elements of information should be retained for them:

Employee number
Department number
Credit card number (for company credit cards used by individuals)

Invoice/Payment File

Every invoice, payment, and adjustment gets posted to the invoice payment file. For balance forward systems, these items are posted in chronological sequence and are identified by the customer number. For open item systems, payments and adjustments are tied to invoices, which are in turn identified by the customer number.

The invoice/payment file needs to have at least the following data elements:

Customer number
Invoice number (for open item systems)
Transaction type (invoice, payment, bad debt, etc.)
Transaction date
Posting date
Amount
Description
Document number for payments

This file is periodically purged in both open items and balance forward systems. In open item systems, the purging is done when closed or paid off items are removed from the file. In balance forward systems, the detail is dropped during the periodic processing as detail is summed into a balance forward. Often the balance forward record is retained on the file as if it were an individual transaction.

Policy Master File

Within a single company there may be more than one set of receivables being administered. If more than one division has accounts receivable, they are likely to be handled separately. If each division has its own accounts receivable closing cycle with different past due policies and bank accounts, then the package needs to store these characteristics as parameters for the accounts receivable processing. The result is a policy master file.

The policy master file contains all of the characteristics that define accounts receivable for particular entities. These items may include the general ledger account numbers for cash and accounts receivable, discounts given, and sales tax. They may include a list of past due messages to be printed on statements for clients. (These messages vary from company to company, region to region, and even time to time.) In addition, the policy master should carry the cycle closing dates and bad debt and small balance writeoff instructions.

Anything that can vary from organization to organization should be included on the policy master. As a rule of thumb, the more that can be input as data or parameters to the policy master, the more setup time will be required initially, but the less maintenance time will be needed over the life of the package.

ACCOUNTS RECEIVABLE FUNCTIONS

Having discussed the basic approaches to accounts receivable and the file structures that are employed, we can now review the essential functions found in accounts receivable packages.

Cyclical Processing

Companies with large customer files often split them into separate cycles to spread the load of work throughout the month. This avoids concentrating it at the month end. This also spreads the cash flow throughout the month.

Utility companies have 20 or more cycles of billing for their customers. Each cycle has a distinct set of customers. Thus while 20 cycles will be run in a month, no customer is billed more than once. Customers can be divided into cycles based on account number, name (all of the A's through Ae's), or even zip code. The goal is to make the split as even as possible.

If a company has a large volume of customers, it should consider cycle billing. Cycle billing eases the month-end backlog by spacing mailings throughout the month, spacing payments throughout the month, and spreading out account collection and follow up. Nearly all accounts receivable packages can do this.

Inquiry

Accounts receivable packages have the best reason of any of the applications for being implemented as on-line systems. This is particularly true for retail applications. An on-line accounts receivable package can be interfaced to a point of sale (POS) system to immediately verify credit and update the account to reflect new purchases.

Commercial accounts receivable can provide on-line access to customer account balances. During order entry, customers can be reminded of their outstanding balances. Credit can be verified before accepting the order. At the shipping desk, it gives final control over shipments. If it takes two months for an order to go from entry to shipping, the credit extended when the order was placed may no longer be valid.

On-line systems are equally valuable for cash application. The goal is to move cash payments as quickly through the business and to the bank as possible. No company wants to hold up the deposit of a check for someone to make a batch cash application. On-line, it can be done immediately.

Most of the considerations for on-line systems are the same for all financial applications. For this reason, on-line applications are covered separately in Chapter 14.

Billing Interface

An accounts receivable package will probably not do billing, although some accounts receivable packages offer a billing module. Instead, billing usually is handled by a separate order entry or invoicing system. The information on the invoices generated from the billing system must be fed into accounts receivable.

Like general ledger interfaces, billing interfaces are not standard across the industry. They all contain similar data elements, but each has its own format. Reformatting interface files is no problem as long as the proper elements are present. These elements include:

Customer account number
Date
Invoice number
Description
Amount

Cash Applications

Cash applications have already been described, including the differences between open item and balance forward accounting. There are some other critical issues when considering cash application schemes.

The application of cash must be fast and easy. It is done often and it must not hold up deposit of checks and cash. The package must control the accuracy of the amounts (with batching if possible) and should validate the accounts or invoices against which the payments are applied. This control is essential to assure that the accounts receivable balances are valid.

With an open item system, there is a problem in applying cash or deposits for invoices that have not been processed. There is no open item against which to post the cash. Any package worth its salt should allow posting of "unapplied cash" against a customer's account. The package can use a dummy invoice if necessary, but a specific unapplied cash transaction is even better.

There are several types of cash payment transaction. A company may receive cash, checks, money orders, credit card vouchers, direct deposit transactions, lock box payments, and even payments in trade. A package must keep track of these different types of payment separately and provide totals on the cash receipts report and the general ledger interface. A good accounts receivable package will provide for these different types of payment. It cannot, however, identify every possible type of cash transaction. Instead, these definitions should be made parameters on the policy master file, along with the associated general ledger account numbers.

Miscellaneous Cash

Companies receive cash payments besides those applied directly to accounts receivable. These cash payments are known as miscellaneous cash receipts. They include reimbursement from employees, cash credits from vendors, rebates, and a host of other items. The same cash receipts clerk who applies accounts receivable cash payments and makes up the daily deposits usually handles these miscellaneous cash transactions too. This means a package should handle these payments as well. This way, all the cash received by a company is reported on the same cash receipts journal.

For a package to handle miscellaneous cash, the cash applications module must accept payments to a dummy account (called miscellaneous cash). This dummy account must not produce statements or end up on the aged trial balance. An even cleaner solution is for the package to have a special transaction just for miscellaneous cash.

Finance Charges

Nearly all retail credit and a growing number of commercial accounts receivable applications require calculating finance charges. Although this sounds as simple as rate times amount, it is tricky. The rates should be parameterized in the policy master so that they can be easily changed. In addition, the rates may vary from state to state. Most states have usury laws that forbid interest to be charged above certain levels.

It gets more complicated. Most companies have a minimum interest charge. (This should be a parameter too; it will change with the interest rates.) In addition, the finance charges may be graduated, depending on the balance. (For balances over $1000.00, the finance charge may be 15% per annum instead of 19.2%.) What happened to the simple calculation of rate times amount?

Small Balance Write-Off

Beyond a certain point, it is fruitless to attempt to collect a small balance from a customer. What is the point of repeatedly sending statements and notices to a customer who owes 35 cents? Even ignoring the cost of the computer and accounting resources used, the postage alone justifies writing off balances below a certain amount.

Probably the height of absurdity was reached (and may remain unequaled) when a credit card system produced a statement for $0.00. Not only did it produce the initial statement, it did not give up there. The bewildered customer received a series of past due and increasingly threatening notices that the account was to be turned over to collection. Finally, in desperation, the customer sent in a check for $0.00. The system was finally satisfied.

The more sophisticated accounts receivable systems have a small balance write-off feature that allows organizations to request that balances below a user-specified amount be written off after a specified time period. These parameters belong on the policy master file.

Bad Debt Write-Off

Unfortunately, not all accounts receivable are paid off. And, good as they look on balance sheets, a company must recognize the inevitable and write-off the amount. This write-off is similar to a cash payment, but it does not affect the cash receipts journal. It is treated as if a payment were received; unfortunately the payer is the payee.

Aged Trial Balance

The most important document produced for the accounts receivable clerks is the aged trial balance (ATB). This report lists outstanding balances and categorizes them into aging categories. Typically these categories are current, 31 to 60 days, 61 to 90, 91 to 120, and beyond. The categories, the selection criteria for the report, and the sequence of it, are all parameters in the better accounts receivable packages.

Several ATBs must be produced. At least one ATB should contain all amounts on file. An ATB should also allow accounts to be selected for reporting. If a company has 100,000 customers, an ATB that lists only those customers with balances over 60 or 90 days is more useful for collection than a full ATB. The selection criteria might include a total balance amount, amounts for any of the aging categories, customer type, and date of last payment.

The ATB spreads the balance over various aging categories. While there are some de-facto standards in business, many companies use their own categories, which may be more or less than the standard. For example, a small retailer may consider any debt over 90 days as a bad debt and may wish to lump together all amounts owed over 90 days. Conversely, aircraft or boat manufacturers that sell to foreign governments may regularly have good debt that is more than a year old. These manufacturers probably want categories that are larger (60 days) and also want them to extend out to six months or even a year.

A large ATB is most useful when it is in a convenient sequence— something besides customer account number. Alphabetic sequences are popular, but other sequences can be useful. (Customers whose names begin with A get more follow-up calls for bad debts than customers whose names begin with Z because the clerks never have the time to get to them.) The ATB can be sorted in descending order on outstanding balance, or it can be sorted by sales territory.

All of this flexibility should be parameterized in a package. That is, the ATB report should be one that can be requested with any of the characteristics desired, and there should be a way to change these characteristics as often as needed.

Statements

As important as the ATBs are, the statement is still the most important output of an accounts receivable package. The statement collects moneys for a company. Most companies print their statements on special forms. This allows information and terms to be preprinted on the form itself, but it presents a printing problem similar to that of printing checks for accounts payable and payroll. Can the package accommodate the preprinted forms? If the package is inflexible, it is easier to change the form than to change the package.

Some packages have a separate report writer to generate statements. These report writers can print about any form that might be designed. Parameters specify where data are to print on the form, the formulas to use in calculations, and where items are to be totaled. Whichever way the statements are generated, the user must decide several key issues: the sort sequence, the cycle, and whether credit balance statements are generated.

Monthly Clearing

The periodic clearing of closed items usually is done monthly, but it should be at the user's option. Some companies use other billing cycles, and they may want to retain closed items for a longer period.

Balance Forward Processing

Balance forward processing accumulates detail data into a balance forward total and purges the detail records from the file. Like clearing for open items, the purging should be at the user's discretion.

General Ledger Interface

Accounts receivable, like accounts payable, can be on a cash or accrual basis. On a cash basis, the accounting is simple. No posting is done when the amount is invoiced. When a payment is made, the sales account and sales tax are credited, and the cash and discounts taken accounts are debited. A more complete discussion of cash and accrual accounting is contained in the next chapter.

Accrual accounting is more involved. When an invoice is first entered, sales and sales tax are credited and accounts receivable is debited. When payments are received, the receivables account is credited and cash and discounts given are debited.

A package must also account for small balance and bad debt write-offs. The more sophisticated packages calculate and post to the "provision for bad debt" account.

The accounts used vary from organization to organization and transaction to transaction. (The lockbox account may be different from the checking account.) This information should be parameterized on the policy master file for easy update.

Chapter 12
Accounts Payable
Packages

The purpose of an accounts payable system is to pay vendors in a controlled, timely, and efficient manner. At the same time, accounts payable should perform the necessary accounting for general ledger and do 1099 tax reporting. Accounts payable may also provide cash forecasting, take advantage of vendor discounts, and prepare detailed expense summaries.

BASIC APPROACH

The basic approach to accounts payable is similar to that of personnel/ payroll. Accounting policy is defined for an organizational unit so that a single system can accommodate the diverse policies of a large multifaceted company. Approved invoices are fed into the system, along with their distribution detail. The package obtains vendor information from a vendor's file, calculates the payment, and schedules it. (The scheduled payments of individual items may be overridden.) When the payment for an item is due, the package prints checks for it. The invoice distribution detail is summarized in a transaction file and forwarded to general ledger. The vendor history is updated, and the cycle is complete. It sounds simple.

FILE STRUCTURE

With payroll, there is one master file. With accounts payable, there are several master files, at least in the logical sense. Depending on the package, several logical files are combined into physical files. However, what is important here is the logical concept of the data, and so we will approach the files as though they were separate. Accounts payable has a vendor master file, an open invoice file, a distribution file, a history file, and a policy master file.

Vendor Master File

This file contains all of the demographic information about the vendor, including name and address, as well as some history. Most important, it contains the vendor's discount terms, such as 2% and 10 days. The package uses the information on this file to calculate the date and amount of payment, to prepare checks, and to print 1099 tax forms.

A package carries a great deal of information about the vendors, some of which may not be needed.

Vendor SIC (Standard Industrial Code)
Vendor bank account number (for direct deposits)
Vendor contact name
Vendor contact phone number
Vendor short name
Maximum invoice amount
Vendor discount grace days
Vendor classification (user defined)
Vendor 1099 classification
Purchase order required flag
Separate checks per invoice flag
Vendor address (optional)
Multiple discount terms
Discount terms (optional)
End of month terms

The vendor data require a lot of input, which is wasteful if the vendor is paid only one time. Most packages provide for one-time vendors. This feature is described later in this chapter. Most packages also offer a section for user-defined data, although the user-defined data are not as extensive as in a personnel/payroll package. User-defined data are used to code special information about vendors for reports. The information is for a company's use only. The package itself ignores it.

In many companies, there are employee payables, as well as trade payables. An accounts payable package handles employee payables, such as travel and expense reimbursement, by treating the employees as vendors. To do this, the vendor master file needs some additional data elements that apply only to employees. These elements include:

Employee department number
Credit card numbers
Employee number
Employee classification

Open Invoice File

The open invoice file contains all outstanding invoices, including those with partial payments and credit memos applied against them. This file is the heart of a package. The whole payment cycle is based on its data.

Usually the information in this file corresponds to the heading information found on an invoice plus a summary of any payments or credits. The data may include the following elements:

Vendor number
Organization code (the specific organization within the company that is responsible for the invoice)
Invoice number
Invoice date
Purchase order number
Date of entry into the system
Terms (overriding the vendor master information)
Scheduled payment date
Invoice handling code
Accounting period date
1099 code
Use tax code
Invoice amount (merchandise, freight, tax, discount, etc.)
Payments
Credits

Depending on the package's ability to override vendor options for individual items, such as terms and bank accounts, this record will have more or fewer data items in it.

Distribution Item File

Each invoice carries with it some detail distribution to allocate the invoice data to various accounts, organizations, and projects. This is essential for proper accounting of accounts payable expenses. A simple invoice may have only one line of detail distribution; a complex invoice may have hundreds. Each distribution record must carry enough information to identify the line, tie it to the proper invoice, and post to the general ledger. The information will probably include:

Line number
Invoice number
Vendor number
General ledger code
Organizational code
Project/job code
Part number/product number
Quantity
Unit of measure
1099 code
Hold code
Amount
Description

Part number, quantity, and unit of measure may be unnecessary—depending on the business—although they may be useful for reporting.

History File

Once invoices are paid, they are moved to the history file. This file retains history for reporting. It is also used to reverse checks or payments made. Without a history file, all of the data from the original invoice would have to be reentered to reverse all the accounting entries. The information also provides an audit trail.

The history file is usually in the same format as the open invoice file. In many packages, all of the data reside on one file. However, the history file includes payment information such as date, amount, and document number. Information in a history file is purged periodically of old items. This purge should be elective rather than at some fixed time such as fiscal year and calendar year end.

Policy Master File

Most packages provide for different styles of doing business by para-meterizing the policy in a master file. Policy master files contain ev-erything from checking account numbers and cycle dates to the policy for taking discounts.

In reviewing a package, check the level in the organizational hier-archy that specifies the policy. If two divisions have different bank accounts, does this mean that the package treats them as totally sepa-rate entities that cannot be consolidated and cannot share the same vendor master file?

Other Data

Besides the files mentioned, many accounts payable packages main-tain other data in files and tables. These data may include organiza-tion codes, general ledger accounts, project codes, part numbers, and employee numbers. It would be nice if all of this reference informa-tion could be obtained from the other systems that maintain them, but the interfacing is complicated and cannot be done in a general way. Instead, most packages offer a good compromise. The data are en-tered, albeit redundantly, and maintained in the accounts payable sys-tem itself.

ACCOUNTS PAYABLE FUNCTIONS

Besides printing checks and 1099's, accounts payable can do a host of functions.

Scheduling Payments

Given the information on the vendor file, the policy master, and the open invoices file, accounts payable must schedule an appropriate payment date for each outstanding invoice. This calculation is quite sophisticated. The package should consider the company policy on seeking discounts, whether the vendor offers discounts, and the status of the individual invoice. The package should recognize when a dis-count cannot be taken and pursue the next most prudent course of action. (If the payment cannot be made in 10 days, wait until 30.)

There should be a way to override individual invoices in order to schedule their payment later or upon some input. A more sophisticated system of scheduling may be needed to consider not only discounts and terms, but also the amount of money available and perhaps even the vendor classification. (The A vendors have top priority, B vendors next, and so on.) The package should recognize that some vendors have a grace period for discounts, some always allow discounts, and some are strict, to the day, about their discounts.

Once accounts payable has scheduled payments, there needs to be a way to see what it intends to pay to allow someone to intervene. That leads to the next topic, prepayment registers.

Prepayment Register

Before a package prints the checks scheduled for payment, there should be an option to review the list. This is often called a prepayment register, or projected payment list. It lists the vendors in sequence, and the items that are scheduled for payment. Although there often is not enough time, the disbursements supervisor can review the document and flag any items that should not be paid. This information is input as a hold on the individual invoices. There may also be a need to hold items by vendor, in addition to holding by invoice.

The prepayment register shows the cash requirements for the next accounts payable cycle. It would be useful to also forecast the cash requirements further into the future, based on the outstanding items currently in the system. This leads to a cash requirements forecast.

Cash Requirements Forecast

The cash requirements forecast is based on the status of the open items currently on file. It predicts the cash requirements according to the final payment date for each invoice. There may be a need to run the forecast with and without the discounts taken in order to determine the way that maximizes the use of cash.

Discount Calculations

A package must calculate discounts and accept discounts that have been input. The calculated discounts are based on the vendor's terms. Discounts may also be overridden on individual invoices. Some vendors honor discounts taken a day or two late, and the package should accommodate this.

Manual and Void Checks

No matter how perfect a package is, checks must occasionally be written by hand. If it is Tuesday afternoon and the CFO can save $5000 on the purchase of a $60,000.00 piece of equipment provided that a check is written that afternoon, the CFO is not going to wait until the Friday accounts payable run. A manual check will be written. Then, the details of the invoice and payment must be entered into the system for proper accounting.

Occasionally, checks must also be voided. The ideal is to enter just the check number and have the package automatically reverse the detail. At a minimum, the package should accept the check information and any detail required.

Multiple Checking Accounts

In a large company, there are usually several accounts payable checking accounts. The accounts payable clerks direct the payments against the account specified. This affects not only the cash accounting but also the sorting and printing of checks.

The bank accounts may be designated by company, by division, by vendor, or even by individual payments. If a company is generous, it will pay East Coast vendors on East Coast accounts and West Coast vendors on West Coast accounts. If the company wants to maximize the float, it will do it the other way around.

Cash and Accrual Accounting

Accounting is either on a cash or an accrual basis. That is, an item is posted either when it is paid or when it is incurred as a liability. Most companies are on an accrual basis, but cash accounting should not be ignored. A subsidiary that is acquired may be on a cash basis, at least until it is turned around.

An accounts payable package should be able to account both on cash and accrual bases. On an accrual basis, the accounting date on the invoice determines when the item is recognized as a liability. Two entries are made; a debit to expense and a credit to accounts payable. The debit to expense will likely be a series of debits to individual expense or capital asset accounts as listed on the distribution line items. Once an invoice is paid, there is a credit to cash (with the account number depending on which bank is used) and a debit to accounts payable and possibly to a discounts taken account.

The invoice is treated similarly for accounting on a cash basis, except that nothing is done until the invoice is paid. Then a credit is made to cash, and debits are made to expense accounts and possibly to discounts taken.

For both cash and accrual accounting, the package must handle cash accounting for void and manual checks. The accounting for this is identical for both cash and accrual accounting and is the same as the cash accounting for invoices. The entries for void checks are the opposite of manual checks.

An accounts payable package generates detail journal vouchers that reflect either cash or accrual accounting for all of the activity in the system. The format of these transactions is not critical; they will probably be reformatted for the general ledger system anyway. However, the journal vouchers must contain the proper detail. Accordingly, the transactions should include at least the following:

General ledger account
Organization number
Project number
Debit/credit code
Amount
Transaction date
Posting date

Recurring Payments

Many items must be paid every month, month in and month out. They might include rent or payments on installment contracts. These payments are a real nuisance to input each month, not the least because they do not usually carry an invoice number.

Some packages provide for recurring payments. After the payments are initially entered, the package continues to generate a voucher each month and automatically pays the item. This feature is even more powerful when the period can be varied so that it can be weekly, every four weeks, or quarterly. It is also useful to be able to enter a stop date to automatically stop the payments.

Partial Payments

Sometimes an invoice should not or cannot be paid in full. Some packages accommodate this by requiring partial payments to be made with manual checks. The more powerful packages allow partial payment to be made by the package.

Separate Payments for Invoices

One of the virtues of an automated accounts payable system is that several payments to the same vendor can be combined and paid in a single check. Thus a single check may list a number of invoices that are being paid. But there are occasions when multiple invoices should not be paid with a single check. Some vendors insist on separate payments, and combining payments may confuse other vendors. Tax deposits are good examples. To avoid confusion, it is better to pay tax deposits individually.

Check Writing

The vendors offer a number of formats for printing checks: stub beside, stub over, and so on. It is easiest to accept one of their formats, plaster the company's own logo on, and run with it. However, there are some issues that need close attention. Will the system handle printing of checks on multiple bank accounts? Does the check writer separate the output so that different check stock can be used for each account? How does the system handle stub overflow? If there are more invoices to be paid than can be printed on a single check stub, what happens to the excess? Can voided checks be written so that information can be placed on the stubs? Is there a provision for a separate print run of overflow remittance advices?

Bank Reconciliation

Bank reconciliation for accounts payable is almost identical to that of payroll described in Chapter 9. Since bank reconciliation has been covered in that chapter, it can be omitted here.

Chapter 13
Fixed Assets
Packages

Fixed assets packages are perhaps the simplest of the major financial applications. This is because there is less updating activity than the other applications, and because the functions are not as complex. Fixed assets packages are used to compute book depreciation, tax depreciation, capital budgeting, cash flow, property management, insurance coverage and claims, and inventory of capital equipment.

The selection of a fixed assets system requires the participation of several groups. Generally it is limited to accounting, but within accounting, the capital budgeting group, the people doing book depreciation, the tax people, and the insurance people should participate.

Unfortunately, the task is often turned over to someone with a limited perspective, like an accounting manager. He is concerned with the accounting entries for depreciation but is not aware of or concerned with tax aspects or insurance considerations that the system must address. Frequently this does not surface until sometime in the implementation when the tax and risk management people emerge with their requirements. "Well, golly, how was I supposed to know about the insurance problem. I mean, I was just doing my job. Nobody told me to check with the tax people, either. Someone should have told me."

A fixed assets package might also need the involvement of the purchasing agent, since so much of the information in the system comes from the purchasing department. If the purchasing agent wants to get involved in package selection, a fixed assets system is the place. However, it will be difficult to get him to think about it as a user rather than a purchaser. "Hey, I know a place where we can get a real deal on a package. My brother knows this guy who can get one for us wholesale. And he'll throw in an old payroll system written in 1401 Autocoder."

Since fixed assets is subject to the tax laws, it is important to buy from an established vendor who is dedicated to maintaining the package. Each election year can sweep in major changes to the tax laws on depreciation.

BASIC APPROACH

Fixed assets packages all have the same basic approach. There is a single master file with a record for each fixed asset item, identified by an item number. The records are also identified by organizational entity so that separate reports and run cycles can be used for each entity. The item records contain all the necessary information for each asset, including a description, purchase information, depreciation information, location, and much else.

In addition to the asset records, the packages contain data that define policy. These data identify classes of assets, the organization hierarchy, the run cycle, and the default depreciation method. Such data may be kept in the asset master file or in a separate file. The ideal is to have each company be treated completely individually but still have a single master file containing all the assets. However, retired assets are sometimes kept in a separate file to speed processing.

The basic processing cycle consists of updating the policy file, with a run date if nothing more. This is followed by a maintenance cycle to add, change, or retire assets. Finally, the book depreciation is run. There is a fourth cycle at year end required to compute tax depreciation and to ready the files for the new year.

The fixed asset package will have a report writer. The many reports that may be generated cannot be anticipated by the vendor, and a report writer is essential. However, many of the federal tax reports are standard, and these should be provided with the package.

FIXED ASSET FEATURES

Although fixed assets packages all have the same basic approach, a number of features should be considered in the selection.

Depreciation Calculation

A major consideration in a fixed assets package is whether depreciation is computed for a period and then accumulated, or recomputed inception-to-date each accounting period. The advantage of accumulating the depreciation is that it is easier to keep the fixed assets system in balance with the accounting system—nothing done this period can affect a previous accounting period. It also makes it easier to bring a partially depreciated asset into the system because the package can accept the cumulative depreciation. The disadvantage is that if errors must be corrected in the acquisition date, or if the depreciation method is changed, adjustments must be made to the cumulative depreciation to change the history.

When the depreciation is recomputed inception-to-date each accounting period, errors are automatically corrected when the attributes of the asset are corrected. If someone decides halfway into a year that an item should have been depreciated sum of years digits rather than straight line, the attribute can be changed and the correct cumulative and current period depreciation will be calculated automatically. The inception-to-date method requires that there be some method of locking accumulative depreciation in so that a partially depreciated item can be brought into the system.

This lock-in feature gives the best of both methods. At any time, the current accumulated depreciation can be locked in, and then the asset can begin depreciating again, using whatever method is chosen.

Book Depreciation

Book depreciation allows a company to spread portions of an asset over an accounting cycle. It is done to reflect the use and obsolescence of assets, and it conforms to generally accepted accounting principles.

Book depreciation is computed each accounting period, and the fixed assets package must generate transactions to be fed into the general ledger system. Book depreciation is usually straight line, but the package should have the ability to establish any of the depreciation methods wanted.

Tax Depreciation

Tax depreciation allows the company to deduct the depreciation expense from its earnings that must be reported for state and federal tax. A company has no desire to reflect a reasonable amount for depreciation, as is done for book depreciation. The only goal is to minimize the tax liability.

Tax depreciation usually is generated only at year end. The system should be able to generate the necessary tax reports. The depreciation methods for tax purposes often differ from book depreciation, and they should be maintained separately. The system may provide federal tax reports, but for state and local tax reports a report writer usually is needed because the reports are so varied.

The depreciation itself is complicated and changing. Tax depreciation can be established by individual item, by group, by composite, or by ADR (Asset Depreciation Range). The depreciation method can be ADR, class life, or facts and circumstances. The package must handle investment tax credits, gains and losses on retirements and recapture under Section 1245 and 1250, lease accounting under FASB 13, SEC replacement cost accounting under ASR 190, current cost accounting, and inflation accounting by FAS33.

Asset Information

By its very nature, a fixed assets system keeps track of capital equipment. Each item in the fixed assets system is assigned a unique identifying number for system use. Usually the asset identifying numbers must be unique across different companies, but some packages append the company number to the asset number, removing this restriction. (This causes a problem, however, when an asset is transferred across companies.) The system records other information for each item, including a description, serial number, vendor information, and on and on.

A package should provide for several types of asset. This includes expensed items (needed for insurance, but not depreciated), nondepreciable items (land), leased items, and items that fit none of these categories.

One of the big problems in a fixed assets system is that so much information can be recorded for each item that clerks are constantly busy feeding information and correcting it.

One of the ways the vendors minimize the amount of information that must be entered is to allow classes of assets to be defined, with table values entered that are assumed for the asset unless overridden. A good fixed asset system needs extensive tables if the amount of input is to be held to a tolerable limit.

Even though the vendor will provide more fields in the master file records than any one organization can use, there will still be a need for user-defined fields. Verify that they are adequate for needs.

Maintenance of assets is a large task. Assets can be acquired, sold, retired, partially retired, refurbished, moved from one location to another, or destroyed. Each of these items will require information to be updated in the master file for the assets.

Capital Budgeting

For use in capital budgeting, the fixed assets system should allow the projection of capital expenditures and retirements out into the future for some number of years. To do projections, it should have the capability to account for inflation and also be able to compute discounted cash flows.

Insurance

A fixed assets system may also be used to track items for insurance. There are two uses of a fixed assets system for insurance: plan coverage and losses. For both, the package must know the location, current value, and description of the item. There should be a way to classify the item and also indicate such information as whether the items are protected by water sprinklers.

Editing

One important aspect of a fixed assets system is the ease of input and the adequacy of the editing and error recycle procedure. Since so much information is entered, the system should ensure that it is correct and provide a means of error recycling and correcting the asset data.

Accounting Considerations

The accounting for fixed asset systems is sometimes more complicated than might appear. An asset that is acquired may be carried as an expense or as a depreciable item. There will be an offsetting entry to cash or accounts payable also. Transfers and retirements also affect several accounts. The periodic book depreciation results in depreciation expense and an accumulated depreciation entry. Often the depreciation expense must be allocated across several departments.

All of the accounting information must be passed to the general ledger system in a transaction file. The format can be different from that needed by the general ledger system because it is easy to write a program to do the reformatting. The transactions need to contain the appropriate dates, the general ledger account numbers, the amount and organizational hierarchy, and perhaps more.

Chapter 14
On-Line Facilities
for Application
Packages

By and large, the major packaged systems were designed and developed as batch systems. They are intended to run on scheduled cycles with the input batched and processed all at once. With the widespread availability of terminals and other on-line equipment and the demand for immediate access to information, there has been a lot of market pressure to make applications on-line and real-time.

Besides the desire for immediate on-line access, there is a strong movement toward source data entry. The theory behind this movement is that those closest to the source of the data, the clerks, should be responsible for entering it into the machine.

The traditional data input cycle calls for clerks to fill out forms and turn them over to data entry personnel, who in turn key them onto cards, disk, or tape. Once the input is in machine-readable form, a data control group coordinates the processing of the data by the computer system. If errors are encountered, they are recycled through the entire process.

Source data entry, in contrast, calls for the direct keying of data from a terminal by the clerk who generated the data. This makes a lot of sense for a number of reasons. We all know the children's game where a group of kids are seated in a circle and told to whisper a word in turn all the way around the circle. The word starts out as "dog" but as each child in turn whispers it to a neighbor, it ends up as "cyclotron" when the circle is completed. There is a similar circle in the traditional data entry cycle. What starts out as a pay increase can be lost or forgotten or may end up as a termination. Batch controls will help, but a lot of time is lost anyway.

Forcing the individual who collects the data to enter them eliminates unnecessary paper flow and a lot of confusion. More important, it gives them total responsibility for seeing to it that all input is in and is correct. Even white-knuckle fliers take some comfort in the fact that the pilot is in the airplane with them and shares in their risk.* Source data entry is a good way to share the risk in a computer system.

An on-line terminal connected to a system provides immediate feedback about the correctness of data. Thus the system sees only valid data, and moreover, if data are entered in error, the clerk will see it immediately and can correct it while it is still fresh in mind. This is the parachute-packing approach to quality control. Random parachutes are selected periodically from each packer, and the packer is required to jump with the parachute. Any quality control problems are self-correcting.

Most on-line package facilities were developed later, after the batch systems, and are usually offered as separate extensions to them. These facilities are integrated into the batch system in one of three ways: as data collection systems, as inquiry systems, or as full-blown real-time systems.

DATA COLLECTION SYSTEMS

Data collection systems are the most common of the on-line extensions to applications systems. There are two very simple reasons for this: they are easy to develop and they can be installed independent of the batch application.

Data collection systems are the most limited of the three mentioned. They collect data on-line and do syntax editing. Numbers are edited, check digits verified, and required fields must be present. However, the data are not validated against the master file and a new data element does not immediately update the master file.

Data input into a data collection system are accumulated and held for subsequent batch processing. The syntax editing catches most errors, perhaps over 90% of them. But, because the data are held for subsequent batch processing and not edited against the master file or processed immediately, there are two classes of errors that will repeatedly pop up: validation errors and run-time errors.

Validation errors occur when an input record has correct syntax but does not match up properly with existing files. For example, a request

---

*The Russians are an exception. Their supersonic transport was designed with ejection seats for the pilot and copilot. Although it could be considered a humanitarian idea, it proved unpopular with passengers.

to change the discount terms for a vendor in an accounts payable system is invalid if the vendor is not located on file. Similarly, a request to add a customer who already exists on the accounts receivable file should be rejected as invalid.

Run-time errors are transient errors that occur only in certain circumstances, typically during a batch run of an application. These errors are the most subtle and frustrating to get around. A run-time error might be an attempt to pay a terminated employee. However, it could result from the cumulative effects of several transactions submitted together.

For example, suppose that a payroll system allows advance vacation checks to be requested for accrued vacation hours. If four transactions happen to be input for a particular employee, one voiding the previous payroll check, one representing a handwritten replacement of that previous payroll check, one calling for the normal pay to occur, and one calling for advance vacation pay, several possible errors can occur. If the void check number does not exist on file and is rejected (a validation error), it will no longer offset the handwritten check. If the handwritten check had vacation time on it, it might reduce the employee's accrued vacation to where the advanced vacation check must be rejected for lack of vacation hours available (a run-time error). Such errors are confusing, frustrating, and difficult to trace and resolve.

In many respects, the data collections systems resemble the sophisticated data entry systems on the market today. They both offer data collection, syntax editing, and batching facilities. Both are disconnected from the actual application.

The only real difference between data collection systems and data entry systems is that data entry systems run on stand-alone special purpose hardware while data collection systems run on the same mainframe as the application package or, in some instances, on closely related hardware such as Remote Job Entry (RJE) systems or a network of minicomputers.

Data collection systems are the least expensive of the on-line approaches and offer a number of significant benefits including source data entry and about 90% of the editing required. There are the obvious editing drawbacks already mentioned (no validation or run-time errors are caught), but even more frustrating is the inability to do inquiry.

Once the thrill of having their terminals to do data entry wears off, the end users will wonder why they cannot look at data with their terminal as well. It may take a few weeks, but the clerks are likely to realize that they have become data entry operators. It is a little like having a new tape recorder and being told you can record with it, but you cannot play it back.

INQUIRY SYSTEMS

The inquiry systems represent the middle step between the data collection systems and the full-blown on-line systems approaches. These inquiry systems attempt to compensate for the obvious deficiencies in data collection systems without the complexity of a full-blown on-line approach.

There are some inquiry-only (look but don't touch) systems on the market and the term "inquiry" often implies that the user cannot change data. However, most package vendors who offer inquiry offer data collection as well, so for this discussion we define inquiry systems as "look but don't touch" data collection systems. There is considerable variety and ingenuity in the implementation approaches of inquiry systems, but they generally can be categorized as adopting either a master file or a shadow master file approach.

Master File Approach

Here the user is given direct access to the actual master file on a look but don't touch basis. Depending on the implementation, this access may include display of data at the terminal as well as some rudimentary on-line reporting. In addition, the access to data may be as narrow as a few selected fields or as broad as the entire file. Control of access may be determined by the operator's level of authorization as controlled by a password or terminal ID.

If the user sees the actual master file, this usually presumes that the master file is organized for direct retrieval, and transactions will be validated but run-time errors will not be caught. The master file must reside on a direct access device (disk) and the data stored using a direct access method.

Most validation errors will be caught, but the more subtle ones as well as those that result from run-time conditions will not be. For example, suppose an accounts payable system accepts on-line transactions to add vendors to a master file. If these transactions are edited on-line but not applied until subsequent batch processing, the system can catch an attempt to add a vendor who is already on file. If, however, a transaction inputs a new vendor that is not on file, the transaction will be accepted. Further, if a second transaction duplicating the first is input, it will also be accepted because the first transaction was edited and stored but not actually applied to the file.

Shadow Master File Approach

This approach was developed to compensate for the problems encountered when the master file is not actually updated with data entered on-line.

With this approach, a copy or shadow master file is created from the actual master file. This copy is then used in all subsequent on-line transaction processing and is updated by the on-line entry of data. A new copy or shadow master file is created whenever a batch cycle is run that updates the actual master file.

Let us see how this works. If a transaction is processed for an accounts payable system to add a new vendor to the master file, the vendor record is added to the shadow master file. This prevents the situation described earlier where a subsequent duplicate transaction is input and not caught as an error. By the same token, a delete transaction physically deletes a vendor from the file so that any subsequent transactions referencing the vendor will be flagged in error.

For convenience, the shadow master file records may be only a subset of the data on the actual master file records. Thus instead of all the data on the master file (for some applications this can be tens of thousands of characters), the shadow file will consist of only the key fields (things like vendor number and vendor name) and a selected group of others.

Some hot-shot programmer analysts will look upon the shadow master file approach with disdain. "It's a Rube Goldberg device to forestall the proper rewriting of the system as on-line, real time. Never mind the costs or problems of a true on-line system, it's the state of the art that matters."

The shadow masterfile approach offers a number of advantages. From the user's perspective it looks like an on-line system that immediately accepts and updates data. In addition, even this pseudo–on-line, real-time system, can be implemented almost as independently of the batch system as can a data collection system. In fact, the actual master file may reside on a tape. Finally, because the shadow master file can be a subset of the actual master file, it may conveniently fit on a minicomputer. In this way, inputs, updates, and limited reporting can be handled in the field.

There are also a couple of disadvantages. First and foremost is the fact that the actual master file is not updated and still must be processed against the accumulated transactions in order to reflect the appearance of the shadow master file. Second, all of the editing and validation performed in the batch system must be duplicated in the on-line system. Thus any changes, enhancements, or maintenance must be done twice. If the editing modules are modularized and can be called from both batch and on-line programs, this will not present much of a problem. However, most on-line programs have characteristics that are inconsistent with batch programs, and so it is likely that there will be duplication.

FULL-BLOWN APPROACH

For most installations, the inquiry or data collection approaches for on-line are accepted as a compromise because a full-blown on-line system is not available or is impractical. Few of the systems currently on the market offer true full-blown on-line versions. In most cases, their basic architecture and transaction formats make it difficult to incorporate on-line technology. In addition, much processing outside the actual entry and edit of data is more efficiently and quickly handled in a batch environment.

Many applications are inherently batch applications. Personnel/payroll is a good example. While it may be desirable to enter transactions on-line and inquire on-line as to the status of individuals, calculating earnings, taxes, deductions, and printing pay checks and registers really constitute a batch function. It normally occurs on a cyclical basis: weekly, biweekly, or semimonthly. Of course, there are cases where an on-line payroll system may be necessary, but these are the exception. On demand payroll is characteristic of transient workers, the screen extra's guild, some oil drilling operations, and real estate commissions.

There are also applications that are essentially on-line but have extensive batch reporting functions. Accounts receivable is a good example. Creation of customers, applications of charges, payments, and adjustments should be handled on-line to provide up-to-the-minute information. However, the reporting, which includes statements, invoices, aged trial balances, and dunning letters, is most efficiently handled in a batch environment.

Some vendors may offer an inquiry/data collection system as a full-blown system, and so the buyer should be wary. To qualify as a true full-blown on-line system, a package should exhibit at least the following characteristics:

1. Only one master file should be in use and its structure should support direct access.
2. Input transactions should be edited and validated against the master file and immediately applied against it.
3. The master file should be available for inquiry and reporting on-line.
4. All transactions available to the batch system should be available to the on-line system.

DATA COMMUNICATIONS AND ON-LINE SYSTEMS

Any of the three types of on-line system discussed will require a data communications system (DC) or terminal control program (TCP) in order to run. A DC provides the means for application programs to talk to terminals. Application programs request services of the DC in order to read or write data at a terminal. All of the confusing aspects of sharing systems resources, polling terminals, resolving differences in terminal types, and handling the differences between remote and local telecommunication become the burden of the DC.

There are a number of DCs available. Both hardware and software vendors offer them. Application vendors typically design their systems around one particular DC, but some offer several versions for different DCs and one even provides its own system. In IBM environments, Customer Information Control System (CICS) is a popular DC. Many of the application vendors have chosen it when designing their systems. If an installation already has a DC, it should look for an on-line system consistent with it. Maintaining two DCs is expensive and troublesome.

A DC is necessary to run an on-line system. It is probably not the best idea to purchase a particular DC just because some application package requires it. Instead, a DC should be chosen on its own merits. It will be used by all on-line applications, including those that must be written in house.

SYSTEM SECURITY

The information contained in financial systems is both proprietary and confidential. In the case of personnel/payroll, the information is very sensitive. Inquiry as well as input of data must be controlled.

With batch systems, security controls are essentially procedural—handling the materials outside the computer. Only certain individuals may prepare input forms, which then must be approved before they are keyed. Printed output is burst and distributed by operations personnel according to authorized distribution lists.

The only real exposure in a batch system occurs when report writers are put into general use. This represents a risk because a user who has a passing familiarity with the report writer may create a report (by accident or on purpose) which accesses sensitive data or data belonging to another organization.

Unlike reports that are produced regularly and have specific distribution instructions, these reports are ad hoc and distribution is difficult to control. Because of their ad hoc nature, the report may end up in a form different from that the author intended. In one instance, a report created by an end user was intended to display annual hours worked by individual. Instead, a data entry error caused the report to select and print annual wages by individual. Unknown to anyone, the report then changed from one of low sensitivity to one of very high sensitivity. The report was left on an output counter where users paw through to locate their reports. There was an interested mob crowded around the report before a manager happened by to discover what it contained.

Obviously, operations personnel cannot be expected to inspect ad hoc reports for content to ensure that no breach of security has occurred.

On-line systems present a host of security problems not present in batch systems. For this reason we include the discussion of security here in the chapter about on-line systems.

Security for On-Line Systems

There are two basic questions in considering security for on-line systems. First, at what level are the system functions controlled: by the form, by the transaction, or by the data item? Second, how should operators or terminals that have access to the restricted functions be selected?

Let us look at the second question first: How are the people using the system identified and controlled? At the lowest level, an installation can control the physical connection of terminals to the system and restrict physical access to the terminal itself. Some terminals require the insertion of a key before they operate. This is only crude control because nothing is known about the operator other than the fact that he or she has physical proximity to a terminal and possesses the means of turning the device on.

This is similar to the security systems of an automobile. The presence of someone behind the wheel does not guarantee that the owner is present. The driver could have picked the lock and hot-wired the car. There is no control over what people do once they access the system. Physical controls offer an all or nothing solution to the problem. Puzzle-loving people take particular delight in breaching system security and are not above hot-wiring a terminal.

An installation needs to know who is using the terminal as a basis for any security. Usually, on-line systems require a terminal user to log on prior to any access of the system. This log on requests an operator ID and a password.

Generally, the operator ID represents a single user of the system and must not be used by more than one operator. The password, kept secret, provides the assurance that the operators are who they claim to be. By providing a means of identifying individual users, functions can be restricted to the individuals who are authorized to perform them.

Some systems utilize passwords to determine the user's level of authority. That is, all people with a certain level of authority can access salaries. However, a better solution is to control access by user. That is, only named individuals can access salaries. One good way to do this is to establish a set of attributes for each user who has access to the system. These attributes are stored in an easily changed table that is protected by the system. Thus when on-line functions are requested, the user's attributes are reviewed to determine if the user should be allowed access.

Some systems go beyond controlling access by particular users and allow only certain functions to be performed at particular terminals or locations. This is control by hardware address or hardware port. Each of the terminals is connected to the computer via a particular port or hardware address. Access can be controlled according to these hardware addresses, in addition to any operator ID controls. Thus payroll updates could be restricted to being performed by a payroll operator in the payroll office.

Security control by hardware address adds some physical security but offers a number of drawbacks. Computer configurations are constantly being changed, particularly those involving telecommunications. Typically, these changes are not made by the same people who are maintaining the on-line applications. Thus there is a constant problem of keeping the system up to date. Second, with today's telecommunications systems, the concept of hardware address is disappearing. Computer communication networks are becoming like the phone system—a switching system. Thus the connection between the terminal in payroll and the computer down the hall may be a dynamic one, just like a phone connection where the line used varies from call to call.

Once there is a good handle on who is on the machine and what that person's authority is, the installation must determine how it controls the functions people perform in the system, from input to access to reporting. Ideally, the installation would like to control not only who but where and when any single function in the system is accessed. In practice there must be some compromise or the bureaucracy to control security would be larger than the operating staff.

How are functions controlled? Well, a desirable way would be to control particular transactions. Perhaps one individual may input time cards to a payroll system but is not allowed to change salaries. Similarly, it is one thing to input a new vendor to an accounts payable system and something quite different to authorize a payment to the vendor. To provide this kind of security, controls are needed at the transaction level. That is, controls over who can submit which transactions are necessary.

How is access to data controlled? The installation probably wants to control access at the field level, difficult as that is. Thus someone in payroll may not be allowed to view personnel-related fields, such as medical claims, names of dependents, and insurance beneficiaries. Likewise, personnel clerks may not be allowed to view payroll fields, such as taxes withheld and hourly rate. This gets confusing because there are fields that both personnel and payroll must see, and there may be individuals who require access to all fields. The cleanest way to control access is by having a table of field names with the attributes required to access them. Such a field name control table can also be used for controlling who can update fields and who can use them in report requests.

Besides controlling access to individual fields, an installation will undoubtedly want to control the organizational units that a person can access data for or provide data to. Again, a table is the best way to handle the problem. Just having tables present does not mean that the system will use them to control access. In fact, this is not the kind of modification that can be added easily. It must be an inherent part of the design. Few packaged systems have done a good job of this.

If a package does not have good security control for input and access of data, a good deal of exposure can still be eliminated by closely restricting the use of the report writers. This can be done by manual controls or by writing programs that scan user-written report requests for potential security violations. Both methods have been used successfully.

Security is a problem that will not go away. In fact, it promises to become progressively worse as more information is fed into the computer and as more people gain access to the computer.

Chapter 15
Report Writers

Most financial packages are supplied with a report writer. While the report writer is seldom a make or break item in selecting a package, it is important. Moreover report writers for general use, such as DYL-280, EASYTRIEVE, CULPRIT, ASI/ST, ANSWER/2, The Data Analyzer, QUICKJOB III, and INQUIRE, are important tools in their own right. This chapter focuses on the report writers supplied with application packages, but much the same items are relevant to the general-purpose report writers.

OVERVIEW

Report writers extract information from existing files and create detail reports, summary reports, and even new files. Most report writers have simple language commands to generate reports, although a few have fixed input forms that are filled out.

Data processing people are sometimes reluctant to use report writers. The programming manager might say: "Report writers are too inefficient. I can write a COBOL program that will run a third faster."

This definition of efficiency is a narrow one because it is concerned only with the performance of the computer. Using the same criteria, COBOL is inefficient compared to native machine language. With the rapidly dropping hardware cost and escalating people costs, the time it takes to write programs often determines efficiency.

COBOL programs are at least two orders of magnitude easier to write and maintain than machine language programs. Therefore, in today's environment, COBOL is more "efficient" than machine language. By the same token, report writers are an order of magnitude easier to use than custom COBOL programs. Unless the report writer is intolerably machine inefficient, it is more efficient to use than COBOL.

The report writer command languages often are described as being "user friendly" because an effort is made to define commands in simple English-language statements that make sense to the nontechnical user.

One device used to simplify the language is a dictionary that describes the data in a file. Instead of using technical data processing terms to describe the data in the file, such as relative byte location, length, format, and number of decimals, the user merely references the data desired by its name in the dictionary. For an accounts receivable file, the user might print the customer name on a report by referring to it with a descriptive field name like CUSTOMER-NAME.

Besides helping to name and refer to items of data, the language of the report writer simplifies some complex data processing concepts, such as selecting, sorting, and summarizing data. For example, selecting all employees in a file whose salary is greater than $15,000 may be as simple as:

SELECT SALARY GT 15000

A sort to sequence a report of accounts payable vendors by state and total purchases might be written as:

SORT STATE TOTAL-PURCHASE

Finally, to produce a report that summarizes detail, such as total salaries by department, one might write:

TOTAL SALARY BY DEPARTMENT

Some report writers offer another big advantage in that they are capable of producing multiple reports in a single pass or reading of the master file. Stacking several reports and producing them in one pass through a file can save time and computer costs.

There are two basic types of report writer: detail/summary and matrix. Some applications require more than one report writer to fill all the reporting needs. One should be aware of the different report writers, how they work, and what they do in order to evaluate whether they will meet the needs.

DETAIL/SUMMARY REPORT WRITERS

This is the most common type of report writer. It also can emulate much of the output of the matrix report writers (though very inefficiently by comparison, as we shall see later.) Detail report writers are columnar oriented. (The exception is the special case statement generator described further on.) Records are selected and data are extracted to be displayed and totaled by column. The report writing process can be summarized as: select, extract, sort, summarize, and print. The select and extract phases, which usually are combined, are the most complex. The sort is easy and the summarization relatively straightforward.

Select and Extract

During this phase, the report writer loads the user's report requests into memory and edits them. There may be more than one request, each identified by a unique ID. Syntax errors and missing data names (not found in the dictionary) are flagged and processing continues. The report writers attempt to process every report even if errors are found. In this way the debugging process of correcting the errors is simplified because there is some output with which to work.

Once all of the report requests have been edited and stored in an internal format, the master file is read. Each record in the master file is compared to the report requests to determine if the record is to be selected. A master file record may be ignored by every request, selected by every request, or selected by some and ignored by others. For each report request that selects the record, an intermediate work record is created. If there are 10,000 records in the master file, there may be 100, 1000, or even 100,000 work records created.

The work records contain all of the data items requested by the report request. If there are 1000 data items, perhaps only 10 are extracted for a particular report. The extracted record has a sort key appended—a string of data elements that cause the report to be sequenced according to the request. The sort key contains each of the data elements that was requested in the sort, as well as the report ID. Several reports may be produced by the report writer in one pass of the master file, so the sort must separate out each report.

There may also be created for each report a set of work records that define the column headings and page titles. These work records are used by the subsequent summarize and print phases to format the data for printing.

Sort Phase

After the entire master file has been processed, the work records created are sorted according to the sort keys created in the select and extract phase. This step may be an internal sort or a separate job step, using a sort utility. There are advantages and disadvantages to each approach. Report writers which use the internal sort save Input/Output operations because the work file is not written out and then reread by the sort, but is passed record by record to the sort.

On the other hand, to take full advantage of an internal sort, the summarize and print phases of the report writer must be a part of the same program containing the internal sort. This makes for a very large, almost unwieldy program that might require segmentation.

In virtual storage environments, these large program considerations are less significant than the problem of too many I/Os. The reason for dwelling on this is that the sort constitutes most of the cost of running a report writer. The sort allows multiple reports to be created in a variety of sequences, but the savings in I/Os are lost if too many reports are stacked in a single pass. Here is why.

The sort time for an unordered sort is approximately proportional to the formula

$$n*n^{1/2}$$

where n is the number of records on file. From this, it is easy to see that if a file is four times larger, it will take

$$4n*(4n)^{1/2} = 8(n*n^{1/2})$$
or eight times longer.

This formula is only approximate. In fact, it is closer to

$$n*\log n^2 \quad \text{or even} \quad n*\log n$$

It makes no correction for the limited work space, work file approach in use in today's multiphase or polyphase/merge sorts. In fact, it is difficult to predict sort times for a sort. System programmers can make estimates, but historical experience with similar files are likely to give a better estimate.

Stacking too many reports can turn out to be more than a case of diminishing returns; it can be a case of negative returns. Sorts grow exponentially with the size of the file rather than linearly as with most programs. Thus a file that is twice as long may take four times as long to sort.

With a report writer that produces multiple reports at one time, many I/Os are saved in reading the master file. However, if the work file that results from the multiple requests grows too large, then the exponential growth in the sort begins to overshadow the benefits of a single pass of the master file.

Let us assume an unblocked master file has 100,000 records (un-

Table 1

Master file records read:	100,000	=	100,000 I/Os
Work records sorted:	1,600	=	64,000 I/Os
Detail printed:	1,600	=	1,600 I/Os
Total			165,600 I/Os

likely for payroll but likely for accounts receivable). Further, let us assume that each of a series of reports will select 1600 records from the file for reporting. Finally, let us assume that our sort requires $n*n^{1/2}$ I/Os to sort a file of n records (this is a generous estimate for a file the size of this). Now with these assumptions, we can see the effect of running the report writer with one report, then two, and then four. With one report, the figures shown in Table 1 result.

Now if two reports for the same file are run by using the report writer twice instead of stacking the requests, there are 331,200 I/Os. However, if the report writer is run with two requests, the figures shown in Table 2 result. The savings is almost 50,000 I/Os over running the report writer twice.

Now the report writer is run with four reports. If each is run separately, there are 662,400 I/Os. If two are run at a time, 567,400 I/Os result. Running all four at once gives the I/Os shown in Table 3.

Stacking the report requests has impacted the sort so much that only 44,000 I/Os are saved, less than was saved in going from one report to two. If the requests had been split into two passes, the efficiency would have been greater than by stacking all four requests together. Obviously, if we continue on and stack 16 reports, a point is reached where more I/Os are incurred than are saved.

These examples ignore the physical blocking of logical records, which would affect the I/O counts considerably. However, only the point of diminishing returns is affected. Perhaps instead of a reduction of efficiency at four requests, it might occur at 10 or even 15. The effect remains the same.

Table 2

Master file records read:	100,000	=	100,000 I/Os
Work records sorted:	3,200	=	180,500 I/Os
Detail printed:	3,200	=	3,200 I/Os
Total			283,700 I/Os

Table 3

Master file records read:	100,000	=	100,000 I/Os
Work records sorted:	6,400	=	512,000 I/Os
Detail printed:	6,400	=	6,400 I/Os
Total			618,400 I/Os

One real world example will prove the point. A *Fortune* 500 company installed a payroll package for about 30 organizational entities totaling approximately 10,000 employees. The package had a report writer, which was used extensively. Nearly 30 reports were stacked together and generated with one pass of the report writer. Initially, payroll took 2 hours to edit and compute each week, and it took an additional 2 hours to run the report writer. As the system was more widely implemented, the file grew to where it contained 75 organizational entities totaling almost 30,000 employees. The time to process payroll, that is, the edit and compute, grew from 2 to 5 hours. However, the report writing time ballooned to more than 10 hours. When the reports were split into two separate runs, this time was reduced to 3 hours a run, a savings of 4 hours. Obviously, it behooves one to pay close attention to the performance of the report writer as the system grows.

Summarize and Print Phase

After the work file has been sorted, it is ready to be read, details are printed, and summaries are made. The file is sequenced first by individual report request (by report ID) and then by the sequence within each report. The summarization and printing phase of the report writer processes one report at a time until all reports have been completed. As each report is processed, detail is printed and totals are accumulated. As breaks in the data are sensed—the end of one department and the beginning of another—intermediate totals are printed and the totals are rolled up to the next higher level. Grand totals are printed at the end of each report.

Most report writers can produce output in which no report headings, footings, or totals are created. This is useful for generating transactions or files. For example, a report request could scan an entire payroll file and create the image of a wage increase transaction for every employee in a particular union. The output, instead of being directed to a printer, could be routed to a tape or disk file and subsequently used as input to the system.

Besides detail reports, some report writers produce summary reports. Thus a matrix-type report, such as the EEO-1 report that summarizes active employees by organization, with columns for sex and ethnic background and rows for EEO job type, can be produced. A summary report is prepared, sorted, and summarized by job type with columns for counting each sex and ethnic background.

Features of the Detail/Summary Report Writer

File Descriptions

There are two usual ways of describing the fields in a file: with a file description and on the fly. A file description is written separately, and each field in the file is named, its starting location and length are given, the format is indicated, and the editing and column heading can also be specified. These file descriptions often are catalogued as a dictionary so that once a file description is written for a file, many report requests can use the same file description.

The other way of describing a file, on the fly, does not require a field to be named. Instead, a field is referred to by its starting location and length. This has its advantages for quick and dirty jobs, but it also means that the file description is embedded in all the executable statements, making it difficult to maintain the report request.

Multiple Files

Some systems use more than one master file. If the application has more than one master file, the report writer should be equipped for this. Accounts payable is an example. There may be a vendor master file with demographic information about the vendors, and then a separate voucher master file with all of the outstanding vouchers to be paid. If a report writer only operates against the vendor master file, balances and other information about the vendors can be retrieved, but not the voucher detail. Even if the report writer can access both files, it may not be able to combine the two files into a single report.

There are two types of multiple input file that may be supplied: sequential and direct. With multiple sequential files, the records are merged on some key to combine the records from separate files into a single record. A personnel file and a payroll file might have a record for each employee: to produce a personnel/payroll report, the records from the two files are merged, based upon the employee ID.

When the second master file is a direct file, a field from a sequential master file can be used to look up a record in the second file. If a project file is direct, an employee time sheet can be read in, and the project number can be used to retrieve the project record.

Numeric Capabilities

A report writer should have the normal arithmetic capabilities: add, subtract, divide, multiply, truncate, and round. In printing a column, there should be a way to specify a formula, the location of the decimal place, and the rounding. If an arithmetic formula cannot be specified, but only single data elements can be, the report writer should provide temporary work fields that can contain the result of arithmetic computations.

Detail Versus Summary Reporting

Both detail and summary reports may be needed. Summary reports that suppress detail and print totals are popular with managers who do not want to be bothered with the detail but wish to see the bottom line. Be sure that the report writer has the summarization feature and check how many levels of summarizations are available. Four levels may seem sufficient, but if a report is created with subtotals for employee, shift, department, building, plant, division, and corporation, six levels are required.

Multiple Output Print Files

With distributed data processing, a report writer needs to direct output to multiple output files. If several divisions each receive their own reports (and no one else's), the report writer must generate separate reports in separate files in order to transmit them to the remote locations.

The multiple output feature is also used to print different forms. One report may print on one-part paper while the rest may print on four-part paper. Report writers solve the multiple output problem by directing output to one of several files.

Multiline and Long-Line Reports

The normal printed report is 132 characters wide. However, with the introduction of laser technology, longer print lines are possible. Most report writers are limited to a 132-character-wide line and cannot take advantage of the wider formats. Because it is often difficult to compress all of the information into a 132-character line, most report writers offer a multiple-line format. That is, more than one line is printed for a single detail record. By staggering the column headings, more columns are effectively created than will fit on a normal page. There is usually a limitation on the number of detail lines per record, but legibility more often, is the limitation. Too many lines per detail record make it difficult to follow columns, even if they are staggered.

Exploding Detail Records

Some report writers can explode a detail record to create multiple detail lines in a report. Unlike creating multiple print lines as described above, this creates multiple sets of lines as if the same record had been read several times.

Here is an example. Suppose there is a history of salary increases contained in each employee's personnel/payroll record. The history can stretch from one occurrence (the employee's initial and current salary) up to 10 occurrences (including each of the last nine increases). The number of occurrences in each record depends on the employee's longevity and frequency of raises. If someone wants a detail report showing the salary increases by job title, the report writer must print a line for each salary increase within a record rather than a line for each record.

The multiple print line format described above does this. It would print a line for each salary increase for each employee, but this would not be a very readable report. A better way is to sort each salary increase (no matter for whom) and list them in sequence by job title. By exploding the detail record to create a separate record for each element of history for each employee, the report can be produced. This is a very powerful feature, particularly when there are elements that can occur multiple times, such as salary history, job changes, and medical claims.

Use of Literals

Literals, or predefined character sequences, often must be printed in reports. Column headings are a good example. The heading VENDOR might be printed above a column of vendor names on an accounts payable report. Literals frequently are printed in the body of reports for row headings.

If there are multiple lines of output for a single record, a prefix such as CITY, ZIP CODE, or HOME PHONE makes the report more readable. Or there may be a need to print a description rather than a code contained in some field.

Access to User Tables

Many of the data in master files are in coded form. Department numbers mean little without names, as do discount category codes, EEO codes, job classifications, and a host of other abbreviations that are used. Tables of these coding structures may be maintained which equate the codes with a literal description. If the report writer is capable of inferring data from tables, it makes reports much more readable.

Some report writers can access user tables. A few even let one designate when the inference is to be performed—at the point the record is selected or the point at which it is printed. This can save a lot of access to the tables (here is where I/Os rear their ugly head again). If a report is sequenced in department number order and the tables are accessed when printed, the access need be performed only when the department number changes and not for each detail record as it is processed.

Access to Portions of Fields

Some report writers allow fields to be accessed or printed only in their entirety. Sometimes only a portion of a field may be wanted, such as an employee listing in which the first and middle initials rather than the full first and full middle name are to be printed. To do this, there needs to be a way to access a portion of a field. The same thing is needed to print an anniversary list and show only the last two characters of hire date, the year. Some report writers can print a portion of a field by specifying the beginning position within the field and the length.

Other Forms of Output

One of the most powerful uses of a report writer is as a transaction generator or file generator. If the page headings and totals are suppressed, the detail lines of the report can be generated as records or transactions in a file. The report writer is especially useful if it generates lines or records that have lengths other than 132. Many report writers can generate alternate output that is 80 characters long, the length of most input transactions.

Automatic Composition and Column Headings

Some report writers are "user friendly" enough that they offer automatic composition features and even automatic column headings. The automatic composition feature relieves people of the burden of determining the print spacing. The data to print in columns are merely specified, and the report writer determines the report layout. It determines the length of data in each column and automatically totals these lengths to determine how much space to leave between columns. If necessary, it creates two detail lines instead of one.

This feature is best for quick and dirty or ad hoc reports. More permanent reports must usually be laid out so that they are consistent in format with the other reports that users are accustomed to seeing.

Besides automatic composition, many report writers offer automatic column headings. For this, the data dictionary contains a column heading with each field definition, and this column heading is printed on the report. Again, this is most useful with quick and dirty reports, which are essentially listings. If a column is created that represents a computation of other fields, a name must be supplied for the column headings. Unfortunately, most of the report writers do not allow one to mix modes. That is, one cannot request automatic composition and also request that a field be printed in a particular location.

Statement Generators—A Special Case of the Detail Report

Statement generators are another type of report writer. Statement generators operate similar to detail/summary report writers, but they are not columnarly oriented. Their basic function is to take an output mask and plug data from detail records into it. Usually this mask is printed for each detail record selected. The mask may take the form of a paycheck, a personnel benefits statement, a letter, or even an account statement.

Instead of just producing a few lines of output for each detail record selected, a page or more of output in any format is produced. Arithmetic computations may be performed to fill in some of the blanks in the mask, but there normally is no subtotaling, summarization, or control breaks.

Rather than producing normal business reports, statement generators print checks, letters, or any other output in which a skeleton format is repeated for each record. The statement generator is most useful when it can generate any number of lines in a mask, such as for a multipage form letter or a large personnel benefits statement.

MATRIX REPORT WRITERS

The second major type of report writer is the matrix report writer. It creates fixed format matrix style reports with predefined rows and columns. A financial statement or profit and loss statement are perfect examples of this style of report. Neither varies in length, but they always carry the same column and row descriptions, which identify various totals.

Matrix report writers are rare as general-purpose report writers. They are, however, fairly common as features of general ledger systems. Normally, only general ledger systems need this type of report writer, but they can be useful for any matrix-type report. Many of the government-dictated personnel reports are matrix reports.

Because of the type of report produced, matrix report writers operate differently from detail/summary report writers. Rather than select, extract, sort, summarize, and print phases, matrix report writers have pass, cast, summarize, and print phases. Normally, all the phases are within a single program, and, as with the detail/summary report writer, more than one report can be generated in one pass through the master file.

Pass and Cast

First, the report formats are read into memory, edited, and stored. There may be more than one format, but each is edited separately for syntax errors. Then processing of the master file begins. As with the detail/summary report writer, every attempt is made to process a report request even if errors are discovered.

Each format is stored as a "worksheet" internally. These formats work much like a spreadsheet does in the manual environment. As each record is read, it is compared to the report request to determine into which columns and rows data will be added. Thus the report writer passes through the master file and casts detail data into row and column positions: much as mail is sorted and accumulated into cubbyholes in a small post office.

At the end of the master file processing, each of the cubbyholes for each of the reports contains the accumulated totals of the records processed. No sort is needed because the cast has already ordered the data. Now it remains only to do any other summarizations specified, such as column and row totals and percentages, and then to print reports.

Table 4

Master file records read:	10,000	=	10,000 I/Os
Work records sorted:	10,000	=	1,000,000 I/Os
Detail records printed:	10	=	10 I/Os
Total			1,010,010 I/Os

Summary and Print

Besides directing which records will accumulate into which columns
and rows on the report, a matrix report writer often can total particular
rows. It may sum across certain columns and perform other arithmetic
operations, such as computing the difference between two columns
and storing the result in a third column as a variance. Once these final
summary operations are complete, the reports are printed. The printing is simple—just a matter of sending the internal worksheet created
directly to the printer.

Matrix Considerations

Matrix report writers are much more efficient for matrix-type reports
than are detail/summary report writers because the sort step is eliminated. As noted earlier, a detail/summary report writer can emulate a
matrix report writer, but at a great cost in efficiency and machine resources. A review of the EEO-1 personnel report serves as an example. This report is a matrix, displayed in columns with counts of employees by sex and ethnic code against rows that correspond to job
categories specified by the EEO. Thus the first row, first column may
equate to white male employees in official and manager roles. The
fourth row, first column may be Native American women in official
and manager roles. A detail/summary report writer can produce this
report by selecting all employees, sorting by job category, and producing a summary report by job category. However, a file of 10,000 employees has the I/Os seen in Table 4.

Table 5

Master file records read:	10,000	=	10,000 I/Os
Detail records printed:	10	=	10 I/Os
Total processing			10,010 I/Os

With a matrix report writer, the various rows and columns are defined to specify the accumulation of each record, depending on the sex, job, and ethnic code. Since the sort is eliminated, the I/Os reduce to those seen in Table 5. The difference is staggering—three orders of magnitude. However, before viewing the matrix report writer as a panacea, remember that it serves a very specific purpose—fixed-format, fixed-length reports. It cannot produce listing-type reports whose length is unknown. Theoretically, the matrix report writer can be loaded up with as many reports as desired without compromising efficiency. However, it is limited by the amount of internal memory available to store report formats. Once there are more reports requested than will fit in internal memory, it is necessary to read and write these worksheets to temporary files, and this can be very costly in I/O.

Many of the features of detail/summary report writers also apply to matrix report writers. Data dictionaries, multiple files, use of literals, and arithmetic computations are all important.

Even more important are the interrow and intercolumn arithmetic capabilities. The report writer is most useful if the user can specify any combination of calculations and the point at which the calculations are performed. Unless the user has control over the sequence of calculations, a total of totals, such as a columnar total of row totals, may be impossible.

Literals are much more important to a matrix report than to a detail/ summary report. Nearly every line of a matrix report carries some literal (CURRENT ASSETS) so the user needs the ability to place literals arbitrarily in the report. One major vendor allows literals only in the middle of the page with its general ledger report writer. Every report must have the same format: one or more columns followed by the literal descriptions, followed by one or more additional columns. This may make it easier for the vendor to write the program, but it is certainly not as flexible for the user.

Chapter 16
Selecting a Package

This chapter will lead us into the details on how to actually select a package. The selection proceeds in three distinct steps:

1. The requirements study, which is done to tell what the package is to do.
2. The Request for Proposal, which is done to tell the vendors what is needed from the package.
3. The vendor selection and evaluation, to decide which vendors to contact and to evaluate their packages.

The result of these three steps is that either a package is selected, in which case the contract negotiations and implementation begin or no package qualifies. The latter case leaves three alternatives:

1. A system can be developed internally (or contracted out).
2. An application development package can be considered. Although these are quite new, they have great promise. Chapter 22 discusses them.
3. The last option is to lower the standards and make accommodations to allow a package to be selected, or be resigned to modifying the package. This is where the real make versus buy decision comes in, although it is really a make versus modify decision rather than a make versus buy.

Now, let us begin at the beginning with the requirements study.

THE REQUIREMENTS STUDY

The requirements study determines the problem that is to be solved. Several steps are necessary. The first is to determine who has the problem.

Who Has the Problem?

Problems with a computer system usually grow like a tumor in the body. There is a vague feeling of uneasiness—all is not well. An irritant becomes a problem, and if malignant, a critical problem. So it is with a computerized financial system.

The first step in the requirements study is to determine who has the problems. Are the problems real? People complain about computer systems like they complain about the telephone company, and the problems may or may not be real. Even if the problems are real, perhaps the people should live with them. For example, there are companies with computer systems fully capable of submitting IRS reports on tape in computer format rather than preparing them by hand. Yet they prepare them by hand because they fear that a computer tape makes the IRS's job too easy for auditing. Obviously, not everyone feels this way, but it points out that what appears to be a problem at one level in an organization may be the result of policy set by another level.

The method at this point is to interview people and take notes. It requires digging down into the problem to see if the complaints are real, or whether they are symptoms of deeper problems. For example, are problems in meeting a tight closing schedule caused by inadequate computer programs, or is the entire error recycle process the problem?

Data processing usually is called on first when it is apparent that a system needs replacement. Data processing can be the driving force to determine who has the problem and whether problems are real. But if it is determined that a new system is to be implemented, the driving force or person in charge of the selection and implementation then needs to be identified.

The Driving Force

The next step after deciding to consider a financial package is to identify the person who is to be the driving force. A financial package is not just going to walk into a company and implement itself. Someone must want the change that it will entail. And until this key person is identified and charged with the responsibility, work cannot begin. Who should this person be?

There is a lot that one might wish for, but only one thing is essential. The person must be single-minded in the pursuit of goals. As a rule of thumb, if one wants to get something big going—say, moving a bunch of elephants over the Alps—get a Hannibal.

It should not be a data processing person, as is so often the case. The financial operations of a company that are served by the financial packages are not the responsibility of data processing. The selection of financial systems is too important to be left to data processing alone. DP staff do not have the line responsibility for the system. And aside from the fact that the systems run on the computer, DP people may have little interest in them.

So we come to identifying the responsible person—the driving force. And the definition of responsibility is easy: whose résumé gets sent out if the system is a failure? The person must be that one with the time who is highest in line authority. If no one has the time, scrap the plan to select a new system. It can only fail.

The ideal person to head the project is the company's equivalent of the chief financial officer. The CFO is most likely to have the power, the drive, and the direction to orchestrate the implementation.

The selection of the driving force is the most important decision made in implementing a new system. Even a bad system can be made to work, given a strong driving force. But no financial system can be made to work in a passive or resisting user environment.

It is also important that the person be made responsible for completing the implementation of a new system, not simply for starting it. A system must be pushed from beginning to end if it is to be completed. It has no inertia. If a person pushes to get it started and then stops pushing, it will come to a rest. It is easy to get a system started because everyone sees only the problems of the old system and not the problems of implementing the new system. Then toward the end, people are bone tired and see only the problems of implementation. This is the critical time, and if the person responsible has shifted attention to new problems, the system is likely to fail.

A big let down frequently follows selection of a package. Selection is so difficult that it tends to be viewed as an end in itself. This leads to a conversation such as the following, six months into a package implementation.

"When are we ever going to get our new general ledger system installed?" the accounting manager will say.

The CFO's assistant pounds the table. "What? I picked the package six months ago. I thought it was all done."

"We're waiting for accounting to decide on the new chart of accounts," explains the data processing manager.

The accountant fidgets in his chair. "Yea, but we can't do that until data processing tells us if we can make the conversion the way we want to set up the new accounts."

The CFO's assistant pushes his chair back from the table. "I don't see what the problem is. The hard part has been done. I shouldn't have to get involved in this now. I've got a management by objective program to work out."

Few things are certain, but the failure of this project is assured because it has no driving force.

Doing the Requirements Study

In examining the problems with the current system, a technique is needed that separates the real problems from nuisance complaints. One way of doing this is to start classifying the problems. Real problems fall into three general areas: volume, function, and maintenance.

Volume can be both a manual and a computer problem. As systems age, they often require increasing manual and clerical effort to keep them going. Perhaps the old system is batch oriented, requiring filling out many complicated input forms, and an interactive menu-driven system could speed things up. Or more likely, the system does not maintain some needed data, requiring the data to be kept manually. Software systems cannot wear out, but strangely enough, they show the exact same symptoms of wear as a physical device. Rather than physical wear, software must constantly adapt to a changing environment.

On the computer, a problem of volume may be caused by exceeding the systems limits, such as field or record size, number of codes permitted, or perhaps the system simply takes forever to run on the computer. The latter usually means that there is not a fit between the current system and what it is being expected to do. Even with the astonishing increases in computer speed, a system that is being used incorrectly can run forever on a computer.

Problems of function mean that the system is not doing what needs to be done. Perhaps it never did, but more likely, it once suited the needs, and then the needs changed. Perhaps when the company was small, it started with a payroll system. When a branch office in another state was opened and two state income taxes had to be handled, the company had a problem. One old payroll system collapsed when an employee had an eighth child, and the system could handle only nine deductions. Many payroll systems began failing when employees started earning over $99,999.99 a year. A large bank payroll service required major modifications to files, programs, input documents, and reports when the maximum individual FICA liability went over $1000.00 a few years ago. If the company was unionized somewhere along the way, the old payroll system probably became obsolete overnight.

Change is constant in all companies, and the effect of change can cause financial systems to slowly wear out. Sometimes the process is slow, with growing, chronic pain. Sometimes it is sudden, such as acquiring a new company where a financial system cannot handle two corporate entities.

As things change, maintenance and enhancements are constantly occurring on the old system. Even good systems become bad as they are constantly patched to handle the most recent crisis, and a lot of systems do not even start out being good, especially if they were developed internally. Each change becomes more difficult to make. It takes longer to make the change. There always seems to be some unfortunate side effect when a change is made, which in turn generates the need for more maintenance.

Some old systems, particularly those written by the obscurity school of programming, were not written to be maintained by anyone but a puzzle solver. "You should write programs so that others can take enjoyment from deciphering the intent."

One needs to get at the root cause of the problem to determine what is real. For example, a company manufacturing medical electronics was being driven crazy trying to generate reports being requested by a government agency. The problem was viewed by the DP people as being one of maintenance. The old system was written years ago on a shaky version of the COBOL compiler in which no one trusted such statements as PERFORM or COMPUTE. The program written was almost impossible to read and change.

The user department viewed the problem as one of function. The system was not able to produce the reports being requested by the government agency. Of course, the report requests were a little strange, too. They were so strange that the consultant working on the problem called several similar companies in the area to determine how they were meeting the needs, because it appeared as if none of the manufacturing packages would do what was being requested. The other companies said that at one time they had received such requests, but they had either ignored them or responded that they were impossible to produce, and that they were no longer being bothered by the agency. The problem was resolved, not by implementing a new system, but by policy—such requests would be done only if reasonable; the other requests would be ignored. The requests went away, probably to descend upon some other unfortunate company.

There is a final reason for making a change that needs little analyzing or reflection: someone in authority is insisting on it. The reasons may or may not be valid, but it certainly simplifies the decision process. And the reasons frequently are good because they reflect the conclusion of someone who is in a position to know that the current system is not doing the job. Obviously, it behooves one to pay close attention to such conclusions.

This often occurs shortly after a new executive officer joins the company and gets the feel of things. The old system reflects a way of doing business, and the officer's insistence upon a new system is one way of saying that the way of doing business is going to change. People within the corporation who are not skillful at picking up such signals lose their jobs. Nothing is more frustrating to an executive trying to make changes than to have people who do not really understand that changes are going to be made. The facts will, in any case, sink home in the unemployment line.

Objectives

During the requirements study, complaints about the current system will abound, with all kinds of suggestions for improving and replacing it. It often becomes confusing because there may be no consensus and one user may complain bitterly about a feature that another user cannot live without. A system cannot please everyone; only a clown can make everyone smile.

The way to put things into order is to think through the objectives. People need to see where they are going before they can select a path. In setting objectives, people should push all the detail out of their minds and think about what it is they really want to accomplish. What is really important?

The first thing that comes to mind should be survival; survival *of* the company and survival *in* the company. For example, a small company once put in a new system to replace its old accounts receivable system. After a bloody two-month conversion, the company almost collapsed because it went two months without being able to get out its billings. This can be a very real problem. A new system may look fantastic, but if the company dies in the process of installing it, its benefits are at least questionable. It is for this reason that many data base management systems will never be replaced, no matter how excellent a new system turns out to be.

In making up the objectives, do not overlook the necessary features of the current system. The objectives might be to provide remote, online order entry for an inventory system, but there are many features in the current batch system that will still be needed in the new system.

The next step in setting objectives is to meet future needs. This is even trickier. By hard work, the current needs can be determined. But how can these needs be projected into the future, as they must be because no replacement system is for today? It will take a year to install, and so with the best case, it will begin its life a year into the future. And it will spend the remainder of its life even further into the future. So in a sense, today's needs are irrelevant. It is next year's needs and the years following that are important.

Projecting into the future, even for a period as short as a year, is a hazardous undertaking. In fact, one can only make reasonable guesses. The only certainty about the future is that it will differ from the present.

There are some techniques that can be used, however. The present can be extrapolated to project the future. This has its hazards, because things follow their extrapolated paths only for short periods. That is why the earth is not up to its knees in rabbits, even though extrapolating their birth rate would predict this to occur. We can also look at known future events or predict the impact of events that will occur in the future. Some things can be taken for granted in predicting the future. There will be taxes, there will be inflation, there will be international instability, companies will grow, companies will reorganize, and key people will come and go.

The Delphi technique is another method. Arrange a meeting with the people involved with the system, and simply discuss what could occur in the future, both expected and unexpected, that would affect the system. The meeting is not to predict the future so much as to examine the impact on the system of unlikely or "unpredictable" changes.

The meeting might consider such changes as the Virgin Islands becoming a state (the package must accommodate more than 50 states), 20-digit social security numbers (it is about time for a change), a new calendar (the Aztecs are due for a revival), conversion to the metric system (well, it could happen), or an acquisition that necessitates multiple charts of accounts. Foreign currency can be more of a problem than just the conversion. If yen or lire must be handled, three or four more digits are needed for numeric amounts than are needed for dollars.

One certainty is that nothing is fixed. One company installed a new package to coincide with its January start of a new fiscal year. Then a month later it decided to switch fiscal years to correspond to the government fiscal year, which ended in June. This resulted in a six-month fiscal year. Then the government changed its fiscal year to end in September, necessitating a 15-month fiscal year. It was three years before the company could get a decent quarterly report.

One final note. If the company has a faint view of the future or if major changes are anticipated, either defer obtaining a new system or select a bare bones model that gives plenty of places in which to customize.

Since the planning is for the future, timing is also an important factor. If the company's business is seasonal, a slack period is a better time to implement. Fiscal year end is always a busy time, and yet some systems, especially those that deal with tax, such as a fixed assets system, are easier to implement at year end. If the company is being acquired by another or if the chief executive is being changed, it is probably not the time to implement a new general ledger package. The timing must be factored into the selection.

Constraints

Constraints stand between what a company wants to do and what it is able to do. Cost and time constrain a company to looking at package systems rather than immediately developing its own system. Many things will constrain a system. Time may dictate when it is implemented and what package is selected. It may also dictate how much of the package is implemented initially. Cost may chime in with its limitations. The availability, experience, and strength of the data processing staff and the end users will also determine what can be done. Corporate policy can place important restrictions on any package selection.

And there are other constraints. A computer may be a constraint, especially if it is non-IBM. The distance from particular vendors' field offices may exclude some from consideration and point the selection toward others. The main point of the constraints is to know the limits.

Steps

Since the requirements study is often done by DP staff, the discussion of the steps that follow is directed toward them. If the current system is well documented, much of this information is already available.

Otherwise, the system must essentially end up having to be documented. The steps in the requirements study are the following:

1. Determine who has the problem and if the problems are real.
2. Select the driving force.
3. Review the current system. This includes the following:

   Narrative description of the current system. Write this in end user terms, and describe overall how the system works.

   Data flow. Sketch out how data flows through the system. Identify the source documents and the people who prepare them, the files that are updated to contain the data, and the reports and their recipients that result from the data. Identify the disposition of all the data that flow into the system.

   System flow. Draw a system flow diagram of the current system if one is not available. It should be a broad-brush picture with sufficient detail to enable one to know how the system works overall. The process of drawing a system flow also helps in learning a system.

   Description of the input. Get sample input forms, user manuals, data entry instructions, and procedures.

   Description of the output. This includes reports and transaction files that feed other systems. For reports, get sample copies, distribution lists, and frequency.

   Master files. Get record layouts and file organization, and note where the files are created. Identify all the master files.

   Volume. Get estimates of the input and output volume described above. Estimate the size of the master files and any transaction files created. Also estimate the computer resources used, especially CPU time.

   Schedules. Describe when the input is entered, when the programs are run, and when the output is generated. Note any critical closing dates.

   Manual procedures. Explain where people interface with the system, who they are, and what they do.

   Interfaces. Few systems stand alone, and so the interfaces need to be determined. This includes transactions, files, and people.

   Run costs. Find out what it costs to run the system.

4. Analyze the problems with the current system. Look at not only what is wrong with the system, but also what is right. It is much

easier to spot what is wrong with a system than what is right. However, when a system is implemented, all those things that were right and were overlooked will be critical. Some of these things that are right may be very esoteric functions specific to the organization or industry. Watch out.

5. Look for additional features needed in the system. Just solving the existing problems may not be enough. The actual needs may be far beyond what the current problem appears to be.

6. List the alternative solutions and evaluate them. No problem has a single solution. Often the alternatives are either to modify the old system or to create a new system. Listing the alternative approaches ensures that the first solution that comes to mind is not automatically selected. The discussion should focus on the benefits and problems of each.

7. Estimate the total cost to implement the system, including the package cost and the implementation cost. This must be a rough estimate, but it must be done now to determine whether the project is affordable.

8. Perform a cost/benefit analysis. The previous step estimated the cost of the project. Now the benefits must be estimated in order to determine if the project is worthwhile. The determination is made by computing the return on investment as follows:

$$\text{return on investment} \ = \ \frac{\text{benefits of project}}{\text{cost of project}}$$

Unless the return on investment is over 1.0, the project makes no sense. The cost of a project is easier to quantify than the benefits. If the benefits cannot be quantified, then deciding whether the benefits are worth the cost becomes a subjective judgment. In practice, it may be impossible to calculate the benefits because the service and function of a system are so intangible. One can estimate the cost, and then it becomes someone's decision as to whether the benefits exceed this.

PREPARING THE RFP

A Request for Proposal (RFP) should always be written. It is done for two reasons. The most important is that putting what is wanted down on paper forces one to organize ideas and decide on what is really needed and wanted. It does this not only for the person preparing it, but also for others in the organization. Everyone involved with a new system will have his or her own ideas of what it should provide, and a written RFP is a tool for gaining concurrence.

The second reason for writing the RFP is that it helps to evaluate what the vendors are providing. Good salespeople can make a skilled presentation and convince the listeners that they have a superior product. The written RFP is needed to determine if this superior product suits the specific needs. Without having these needs in writing when dealing with a vendor's sales staff, the initiative is surrendered to them, allowing them to focus on what their package provides. By using the RFP, the focus is brought back to the needs and how well their package meets them.

Writing the RFP takes a lot of time, but the more time spent, the less time the total selection and implementation will take. The investment in time must be made to decide what is needed. If there is not enough time to write a good RFP, the project should not be considered because it will result in a disaster. As a rule of thumb, a person who has not expended the effort to prepare a good RFP should expend more effort preparing a good résumé.

To prepare an RFP, first make a list of the things that are wanted in the new system. Examine the old system to determine what of it must be retained, what must be changed, and what must be added.

It is easiest to see what the current system is doing wrong. Everyone will be able to speak hours on its shortcomings. It is more difficult to see what it is doing right. Much of what it does will be taken for granted, and its importance will not be appreciated until it is changed.

As an example of what can occur, one company doing a payroll selection neglected to take into account a special requirement in their state that people earning standby pay, doctors available on call in this example, were not only paid, but their earnings on standby also went into determining the hourly rate for overtime. Everyone involved in the selection tacitly made the assumption that this would be true of every state, and that all payroll packages would provide it. But since it was unique to a particular state, the package selected did not provide it, and the omission was not discovered until checks were being printed and people began to complain.

It is an invariable rule that there is nothing, absolutely nothing, in the current system that someone does not depend on. For example, some reports produced may appear to have no redeeming social value, but if they are tossed out, a scream will be heard somewhere from the bowels of the organization, as users find out that the report they depend on is no longer being produced.

This is not to say that they actually need the report or that the report should be kept, but only that they will be heard from. At the onset of World War II, when reorganizing coastal defenses, England found that the country was still paying for a person to stand watch over the White Cliffs of Dover to ring the church bells should Napoleon appear with a French fleet. Naturally, the person screamed when the job was eliminated. All kinds of strange things surface when a system is replaced.

By hard work, a list of specific items that are needed and wanted in a new system can eventually be hammered out. The next task is to determine which are needs and which are wants.

Weighted Average

A traditional way separating needs from wants is by a weighted average. Someone might arbitrarily assign a value of 10 to the most needed item, and assign weights from 1 to 9 to all the other items. This method has appeal because it quantifies the selection. Vendors can be evaluated to see if they provide each feature, and then the weights are added for all the features provided to come up with a total. Then a vendor with the highest total is selected.

The weighted average is easy to perform, it has the appearance of objectivity, and it provides a rationale for selection that is quantified. For these reasons, it has strong appeal.

In practice, it is anything but objective. By the time a group of people go through a selection process, they generally know which package they want. The problem then boils down to juggling the weighted averages to make sure the correct package is selected.

The fact is, packages should not be selected objectively. They should be selected subjective to what the requirements are. For example, would the pilot of an airliner assign a value of 10 to having enough fuel on board for a flight, and assign values ranging from 1 to 9 for adequate dinners, drinks, newspapers, and pillows on board? And should the pilot then take off if the total were more than 20? If there is not adequate fuel on board, none of the other items matter.

French Triage System

Another method of determining needs is the French triage method. The French army divides its wounded into three groups. The first are those who will not survive and for them treatment would be a waste of effort. They are set aside. Next are those who will survive even if they are not treated immediately, and they are also set aside. Finally there are those who will survive only if they receive immediate attention. It is to these that the doctors give their attention.

For package selection, the list can be divided into three categories: things that the company must have, things it needs but could live without, and things it would like. The first category would include items without which the package would not be selected. The second group would be features that are not critical but that the company would like. A weighted average might be performed on these if necessary. Finally, little attention need be paid to things that company merely notes in passing.

The Japanese Method

The point was made that often at the end of an evaluation, the selection group knows which package it wants without having to quantify the selection. The group may not even be able to quantify it. This selection process might be termed the Japanese method. It is something that we in the West do not do well: decision making by consensus or as a group. For us, a strong personality usually dominates, and tools like the weighted average are used to combat this.

But it can be successful when a group of people work hard enough on a problem and pound at it enough so that a consensus eventually emerges. The advantage of this method is that it forces people to really think through their needs. A weighted average is easy and people do not have to put much effort into the selection. The group method is also dynamic. The view of the people at the end of the selection process may be very different than at the beginning. Selection is a learning process stimulated by the response of the vendors.

Even when the selection is by the group method, a weighted average may still be necessary to give the proper trapping of objectivity to the decision. If a quantifiable decision is expected, it must be given. Of course, the weights are assigned so that the correct package is selected, and while someone may consider this method to be cheating, it is, in fact, merely a way of validating the weights that have been assigned.

WRITING THE RFP

In writing the RFP, do not use glossy terms or buzz words. Every vendor's package is modular, top-down designed, structure programmed, flexible, integrated, user friendly, and all those other computer terms that mean "something good" and little else.

Never write the RFP so that questions can be answered yes or no. Nothing will be learned because, by a little stretching of a package's capabilities, the vendor will be able to answer all questions yes. Do not ask if a package does something else; it always will. Instead, ask how it does it. The vendor's answer then can shed some light on how the package works. Most packages will be able to do most of what is wanted. What then becomes important is how the packages accomplish what is wanted. This information also can shed light on how efficient the package will be for an application.

The RFP should be written and organized as a working document. Like all documentation, write it to be changed, preferably on a word processor. Double or triple space to leave room for comments and annotations.

Each person must develop organization for the RFP, but the following is typical.

Company Overview

Describe the company in general, its industry, and its organization. Include the distinctive aspects of the company that are causing problems in the system being replaced. For example, if there are five different divisions that barely speak to one another, and five separate general ledger systems are being combined into a single general ledger system for the five divisions, tell this to the vendors. Do not be coy with the vendors. By telling them about the company, they are better prepared to direct their proposal to the problems. Write the description as if it were a case study.

Problem Overview

Describe the problems with the current system and why it is being replaced. Sketch out what is wanted from the replacement system. For example, if the company is going from a batch system to on-line, explain this because it helps the vendors focus on what is wanted. Since this is an overview, it can also be written as if it were a case study.

Deliverables

Have the vendors list what they provide. Ask about things like input forms or artwork for forms. The deliverables usually include the following:

Manuals and documentation
Source, including number of statements and number of programs
Language in which written
User training
Test data

Hardware/Operating System Required

This is especially important with a non-IBM computer.

General Approach

Ask for an overview of the system in enough detail to understand its operation. The items to consider are the following:

Input
Processing
Output/reports
Manual procedures
Error procedures
Systems flow

Master Files

The master files are the key to really understanding a system. This should include the following:

Purpose
Organization
Brief description

Functional Characteristics

This is where the detail of what is wanted is spelled out. It will constitute the bulk of the RFP. Write this in the form of a list, asking how the vendors provide the feature in their packages, and then leave room for the vendor's response. Do not phrase questions like this:

"Do you provide a means of reversing checks?"

The answer will always be yes. Instead, phrase the question like this:

"How does your package handle the need to reverse checks?"

Not only does this tell whether the package has the feature, it also gives some insight into how the package does it. In a subsequent review session this may fuel some further questions to ask the vendor. The questions might be further organized together in the following categories:

Must-have features
Needed features
Would-like features

Ability to Include User Modifications and Hooks

Here the need is to know how far one can go toward customizing the package without violating its integrity or affecting maintenance. Again, remember that the goal is to know not only what the vendors provide, but also how they provide it.

Keep in mind that the RFP may have to be revised. Evaluating an RFP is a learning process, and items missing in the RFP may crop up or items provided by vendors that were not considered may be decided to be essential.

In sending the RFP to the vendors, make sure they are told to respond according to the current version of their system and annotate the RFP wherever they are proposing a feature that will be in a future version. With all vendors, the new, improved, but still off in the future version will have all the features lacking in the current version. These are like political campaign promises and should be taken about as seriously.

VENDOR SELECTION

An application package is not selected. Instead, packages are eliminated, and then what survives becomes the choice.

The first step in selecting vendors is to get a list of them. The DATAPRO and Auerbach publications both publish lists of vendors, and magazines like *COMPUTERWORLD, Software News, DATAMATION, Computer Decisions,* and the *ICP Quarterly* also are sources. Appendix B contains a more complete list of information sources.

Appendix A lists the major vendors of the financial applications packages. These vendors, but not just these vendors, should all be on the list. Add others as they are discovered. Associates and contracts in other companies are also a good source of package vendors.

For any of the major application packages, the list will be about 100 vendors. This is far too large a number with which to work, so the list is pared down by eliminating as follows:

1. Those packages not implemented on the same hardware or system software as at your installation.
2. Those packages with only a few installations—unless someone is familiar with the package or vendor.
3. Those vendors with whom your experience or the experience of someone you trust has been bad. Be sure that the bad experience was caused by a bad vendor or a bad package and not a bad fit of a package. Guard against a good package being tainted because it was installed in the wrong environment.

By now, the list may be down to 10. Write the vendors to request literature. Literature does not commit anyone, and although there will probably be a follow-up sales call, the salesperson will not knock down the door. From the literature, the list may be pared down even more, to perhaps five or so. More likely, there will be only two or three remaining.

Now the selection is getting serious. Organize a selection committee to review the remaining vendors. Make sure that the selection committee is the sole point of contact within the company for vendors. Some vendors, when they sniff out a hot prospect, like to come into the company at the top. This must be prevented because lunches, baseball tickets, and bonhomie do not a good selection make.

Having gone through these steps, open the flood gates and contact the vendors by sending them the RFP. The vendor's salespeople now know that your company is a hot prospect. They will put all the effort into the sale that a commission on $50,000 or more engenders.

When the vendors' responses to the RFPs are received, the list may be narrowed down even more. The list may be no larger than one, but even if it contains only one name, the selection proceeds exactly the same. At this point, an arbitrary best package or vendor is not being selected; the selection is to pick a package that fits the company's needs.

So far, the effort has been essentially that of one person, usually a programming manager from data processing. From here on, the effort must involve both data processing and the end users. The accounting manager, the accounting clerk, and even the internal auditor should participate.

The next step is to let the salespeople make their presentations. The vendors have invested a great deal in their sales presentations, with slides, perhaps music, and sometimes video. The presentation may not do anyone much good, but as a courtesy, someone should sit through it. Later, when a package is selected and the selection needs to be sold to management, the vendor's sales presentation can be an effective tool to use.

After the sales presentation, which does not have the effect of engendering enthusiasm, there should be a larger, more detailed session to go over the RFP item by item. Two people from the vendor should be present: the salesperson and a technical representative. Good salespeople are usually not technically oriented and often know little about the internals of a package. From the salesperson's point of view, this is an advantage. It provides a reason for avoiding questions. The meeting will need a technical person to respond.

There are several other reasons for bringing the technical person from the vendor into the presentation. They are usually not sales oriented, and often give surprisingly candid answers. Their business is to know how the package works, and they have little patience for a salesperson being exuberant about a bad feature.

The technical person's presence prevents the salesperson from ducking questions—questions that might otherwise not be followed up. In the session, watch the technical person. Even if she or he says nothing, sighs, quizzical looks, head snapping back, or chair flipping over backwards are clues suggesting that a question be followed up closely. Also, there is something about the presence of a technical person that seems to make a salesperson more candid.

The following conversation illustrates the value of having a technical person present.

"The tax module is the best feature of our package," the salesman says. "It was written by our most brilliant programmer."

"I'll say he was brilliant," the technician whispers. "Good old Homer. He left a year ago to start his own company, and we still haven't been able to understand how the thing works."

"It's state-of-the art," the salesman continues. "Completely structure programmed and top-down designed with lots of flexibility."

"Yea, Homer missed his calling," the technician whispers. "He should have been a cryptographer. We've had four people trying to figure out how to change the tax module."

The salesman glances nervously at the technician, but continues.

"The response to the new budgeting feature has been fantastic. Over 100 installations have ordered it."

"Yea, great," the technician whispers. "One hundred orders; zero implementations. No one can get the miserable thing to work."

"We plan to have an on-line feature available in a year," the salesman continues, giving the technical person a cutting glance.

"Homer will have it sooner," the technician says under his breath as he lights up a strange-looking cigarette. "He took the design with him to start his new company."

Usually the conflict between the salesperson and the technical person is less direct, but then again, sometimes it is worse.

Representatives from both the end users and data processing should attend the session too. Both should be encouraged to participate and ask questions. Everyone should be reminded that there are no dumb questions. Often what appears to be a dumb question elicits a surprising response from the vendor that tells a great deal about a package.

If an accounting clerk wants to ask "Does it matter when we run the package on our computer? I mean, you have an accounting calendar inside the system that tells it what the period ending dates are, don't you?" Of course they do, and it is a dumb question. But then if the vendor answers, "Right, it doesn't matter when you run, just as long as it is not on Sunday. The system checks the IPL date of the computer to make sure that the package is never run on Sunday." Now the question is not so dumb. (One package actually had such a feature.)

This is one of the reasons for inviting people from accounting to the meeting. They are a fountain of dumb questions. Data processing people know too much and will not ask the obvious questions.

The biggest trap that people fall into in selecting packages is their assumptions and extrapolations. Humans have a great ability to fill in the blanks to assume, to infer, and to extrapolate. That is why Hollywood can save a lot of money in movie props by building houses with just fronts and no backs. However, when this gift is used in evaluating packages, dangerous mistakes sometimes result. If an accounts payable system handles one type of esoteric discount term that one would not expect, do not assume that it handles the traditional ones as well.

Remember in going over the RFP that the purpose is not to disqualify a vendor if the response to a question is not entirely satisfactory. Otherwise the list of candidates will go to zero. Selecting a package requires compromise, and much of the selection process is to find out where to compromise. For this, the vendor's system must be learned well enough to know if it will be a satisfactory solution to the company's problem. Looking for a perfect solution is a waste of time. Some people will never accept this. "Aw come on. Their client list contains most of the *Fortune* 500. The package has got to be able to do what we want. We can't be that different."

After the sessions with the vendor, assuming that there are still vendors in the running, the work is not finished. Ask for two things: the user manuals and a list of local references from similar organizations.

Vendors will usually supply a company with the user's manual, although they may require signing a nondisclosure agreement. The user's manuals are another source of information on how packages work. They let the reader see the system from the user's point of view. They can also answer questions that might occur during the selection process.

The list of references of similar installations is even more useful. Talk to the people who are working with the system. There are two problems with the names that the vendor will supply. First, they are installations that the vendor thinks are successful. (However, sometimes the vendor does not know that a customer is dissatisfied.) Second, the vendor will probably suggest talking to the person who selected the package. This is not the person with whom to talk. The person who selected the package is not going to admit that it was a bad selection.

Someone should telephone the installations supplied by the vendor, and then ask those installations for the names of other installations. They can also ask for the names of the people involved in the day-to-day operation of the package. With a little work, one can get representative installations of the package and a qualified list of names of people using the package who have no vested interest in defending it.

In addition to using the telephone, the selection committee should plan to visit one or two installations. This lets them see the system in operation and talk to various people who use, run, and support the package. They can quickly learn how well the vendor supports the package, weak points in the package, and how well maintenance and enhancements are handled. Often more can be learned about the package's performance and efficiency than by benchmarking or any other means. The group should select an installation in an industry similar to the company's so that the people can talk about common problems to the end users.

People like the accounting clerk should go along on the visit. This gives the clerk an opportunity to see counterparts in other organizations. The clerk will see someone else in a job similar doing it in a different way. This helps prepare for the eventual changes in the clerk's job.

The committee should not expect everyone at the installation visited to be ecstatic about the package because that never happens. The committee should look for significant problems that would prevent the package from being a success in the company.

Select the Vendor

When this point is reached, it should be clear to the selection group which package is to be selected. If not, the effort probably has not been thorough enough. If there are two or more candidates from which no one candidate is clearly better, a weighted analysis can be used to help in the decision. However, this is a bit like someone using a weighted analysis to select from two people which one to marry. It really means that the selection group members do not understand their needs well enough to make any selection.

Change Analysis

The final step after selecting the package but before buying it is to perform a change analysis. This entails scheduling a meeting of all the people in the company who were involved in the selection. At the meeting, everyone can discuss possible future changes and how the package would handle them. The important thing is that it be done as a group. A suggestion made by one person will spark an idea in another. As in the meeting to go over the RFP, there are no dumb questions. A few years ago, suggesting a prime rate of over 20% would have been "dumb." There are no dumb questions in looking at the future.

The meeting should result in a written summary that lists possible changes and how the system would handle them. When changes do occur, the document can be used for reference. On the personal side, it is also an impressive document to pull out when an unexpected change occurs. To have anticipated the unexpected demonstrates competence if not prescience.

SUMMARY

Package selections begins with the requirements study, which lets one write the RFP. Vendors are then picked to receive an RFP. Their responses are evaluated. The vendor's salesperson and a technical representative are invited in to go over the RFP in detail. Other installations are contacted to see how the package operates for them, and then finally a package is selected. No shortcuts should be taken, because the success of a package depends on how well the selection is done.

Chapter 17
Buying the Package

Buying a package ought to be simple but often is not. Most packages are not purchased outright but are obtained under a license agreement that establishes a continuing relationship between a company and a vendor, with rights and responsibilities on both sides. The vendor agrees to provide a system that works and may agree to maintain it. The company agrees to protect the system against someone else's using it or copying it. This ongoing relationship, plus the abstractness of computer software, results in a somewhat complicated contract.

There are usually four groups involved in the package agreement: the vendor's salesperson, the vendor's legal staff, the person making the package selection, and the company's legal staff. The purchase agreement is not something to turn over to the legal staff. The legal staff know law and contracts, but they do not know software. They may leave out some critical items and attach great importance to items that, in software, are silly. They might insert a clause that the package must contain no bugs, whereas a person who knows software knows that no package has ever or will ever be delivered without bugs. The legal staff should be used for technical support. The negotiations should be controlled by the person making the selection. This person should decide what is wanted and then work with the legal staff and the vendor to get it into the contract.

The important thing in negotiating a contract is to get what is wanted in writing. To save time, there is a temptation to come to agreement by handshake. The salesperson often suggests that since both parties are in agreement, there is no need to get it in writing. The opposite is true. If both parties are in agreement, there is no reason not to get it in writing. Once the contract is signed, the salesperson may not be seen again. If a conflict later arises, the salesperson may be working for another company, and the vendor will have little interest in verbal agreements made with a terminated salesperson. They may have little interest in verbal agreements in general.

WHAT IS NEGOTIABLE?

The salesperson will deliver a contract that the company is to sign. The salesperson will affirm that this is a standard contract that has been signed without change by all its customers, and that its contents are inviolate. This is not quite true—in fact, it is probably the exception. Most contracts require some change. The salesperson is not going to let $50,000 or more in sales slip away so that a standard contract can be kept inviolate. Only one vendor is large enough not to change its standard agreements: IBM.

A great many things can be negotiated in the contract. In fact, about the only things not negotiable are the basic package to be purchased, the responsibility to protect the package, and the price. And there may even be ways to negotiate around the price. Vendors cannot negotiate the price directly because they must maintain their integrity with those who have already purchased the package. However, the vendor may be enticed to throw in some extra training or package features. There may be discounts for buying more than one package from a vendor. If the package is implemented on a non-IBM computer or the company must make major enhancements, it may be able to sell these back to the vendor in terms of a reduced price.

The salesperson will not want to change the contract, even for reasonable items, because of the delay and cost that it involves. The company will also not want delay, and so changes should be limited to the essential.

As a buyer of a package, the company may want the vendor to customize certain features of the package or provide additional functions that are needed. Do not expect the vendor to go far in doing this. The vendor cannot afford to customize a package, it cannot afford to maintain customized versions, and it is not interested in adding features to a package if the features can be used only by a single company. Package vendors do not have the inclination or staff to do custom programming.

Among the things to consider in negotiating the contract are ownership, the deliverables, the acceptance, the restrictions, the warranty and maintenance, the liability and responsibility, and even the payment. The standard provisions of the vendor's contract may be acceptable for most items, but usually there will be one or two items that require special consideration.

Ownership

Usually the company does not own the package but only uses it under a license agreement. It may or may not own the training aids and documentation. The contract should clarify whether the company can reproduce them for internal or external use.

Deliverables

The contract should spell out what the company is to receive: source, object, listings, acceptance materials such as test data, documentation, training, and assistance. Once the package is purchased, the salesperson may not come around again, and so if they promised a copy of their presentation slides for the company's use, this should be included in the contract. Since time is critical in any system implementation, the contract should spell out when the items are to be delivered.

A vendor often agrees to supply some number of hours of training. Even if the number of hours cannot be negotiated, the schedule and timing may be. Training is vitally important, but it is wasted if given too early or too late, or if the necessary people cannot attend. Training for the end users is as important as the technical training given to data processing.

The same training given the end users should also be given the programmers. If the programmers know what the system does, they will by implication know a great deal about how the system must work. In addition, it is the programmers who often end up having to train the end users, after the package is installed.

Acceptance

There is always a conflict in acceptance. The vendors will want acceptance to be based on running their test data. The company will want acceptance to be based on the system running error-free in production for some number of periods. It is likely that compromise will be made on the side of the vendors. Sometimes acceptance is based on running test data that the company develops. If so, this must be spelled out in the contract, and the test data to be used must be described. Sometimes acceptance is based on the system adhering to certain specific items in the RFP. If the maintenance contract covers enhancements, an acceptance clause may be put in for the enhancements. The first releases of a vendor's enhancements often cause difficulties.

Restrictions

The contract will limit what the company can do with the system. If it plans to sell the system as a service in a service bureau environment, even if done internally, this needs to be carefully spelled out in the contract.

The vendor will usually restrict the package to run on a single computer at a single location. There should be a provision to allow test runs to be made on another computer for establishing emergency backup, and also run on another computer in an emergency. Always retain the freedom to change computers. At most, the vendor should only require notification of a change. Computers have about a one-year half life today before they are replaced or upgraded. Likewise, the company should be able to move its computer to a new location.

With attached or multiple CPUs and distributed data processing, what constitutes a computer is becoming unclear. If several CPUs are in a network, the package might run on a different CPU each time. Furthermore, the data entry and report writing portions of the package might be concurrently on several computers in a network. Such usage should be indicated in the contract so that the vendor cannot force the company to purchase the package for each place it is run. (If the package is run as a complete system on separate computers, the company will probably have to buy separate copies of the package.)

The contract should spell out whether the vendor can use the company's name in its advertising and as a reference. It should also cover the reverse. The company may want to use the vendor's name itself.

Warranty and Maintenance

The vendor will usually provide some warranty period for the package, after which a maintenance contract must be signed for continued support. The company will want this period to start after it accepts the package. The vendor will want it to start when the contract is signed. This can often be negotiated so that it falls favorably on the company's side. Perhaps the warranty period should be reset in case the system fails. The contract should also specify a minimum response time for maintenance, and whether the company or the vendor pays for labor,

travel, and subsistence. These items should be covered in any maintenance contract, too.

One important item to consider in the warranty or a maintenance
contract is access to qualified personnel when necessary. The vendor's hot line usually is staffed by trainees whose purpose is to screen
most questions from the true technical people. It is extremely frustrating trying to work a tough problem, having to use a trainee as a go-
between. The maintenance contract should also be clear on whether it
also covers enhancements.

Liability and Responsibility

Although the vendors will warranty the product to correct any errors,
they will exclude liability for any damages caused by the errors. The
same thing should apply in limiting liability to the company in protecting the package. If a disgruntled employee makes a copy of the
package, quits, and goes into business selling it, the company would
not want to be held liable. It is unlikely that an employee will copy a
large applications package, but in the area of personal computers, people are shameless in what they copy.

Payment

The vendor will want total payment when the contract is signed, before any materials are delivered. The company will want to defer all
payments until after acceptance. Again both sides must compromise.
Payment should be keyed to events, with portions of the payment
made upon execution of the contract, receipt of materials, training,
acceptance, and perhaps even the end of the warranty period, if it is
short. The vendor will be unwilling to let payment depend on events
whose timing or success rests on the company, but within reason, the
payments can be made as the vendor delivers.

YOUR LEGAL STAFF

The most difficult part in negotiating the contract may be not in dealing with the vendor but in dealing with the company's own legal staff.
The agreement should be passed through them, as should any contract, but the negotiations must not simply be turned over to them.

All professionals view their services as being more important than
any others. The lawyers in a company's legal staff will view the suc-

cess of the package implementation as resting upon the exact language that goes into the package agreement. Thus if there are 12 months in which to implement a package, the legal staff will see nothing wrong in taking two or three months of this to negotiate the fine points. Sometimes one cannot afford to let this happen.

Corporate legal staffs seem to divide into two groups. The first are overextended, and it will take a long time for the contract to get attention. By applying the squeaking wheel theory, one can often force it through more quickly.

The second group presents more difficulty. They are overstaffed, undercommitted, and feel a little insecure about it. Consequently, to show their worth, they will go through the contract word by word, raise hundreds of trivial points, and essentially rewrite the contract. If this is allowed to happen, there will be a long delay. This waves a red flag in front of the vendor's legal staff, and they will feel obligated to reciprocate.

The best way to deal in this situation is for the person doing the selection to know what is wanted from the contract, convey this to the legal staff, tell them the importance of the timing, and monitor it closely. The person should treat the legal staff as a technical support group over which he or she has veto power. Any changes the legal staff initiates should be justified. Eventually, a good working relationship may evolve.

SUMMARY

The important thing in negotiations is to be reasonable. The vendor wants to sell the company the package, wants the installation to be a success, and will do most reasonable things to ensure the success. However, the vendor needs to make a profit too, and if what the company wants to negotiate precludes a reasonable profit, the vendor would rather forgo the sale. None of the major package vendors will need to exchange the prestige of a sale for a profitable installation.

Chapter 18
Implementation

Once a package is purchased, the difficult part has just begun. It's like buying a central air conditioner for a home. One cannot simply take it home and plug it in. The house must be prepared with ducting, insulation, a power supply, and thermostats. The package has been bought. Now it must be made into a system.

Packages have no inertia of their own. There are many steps in the process of installing a package, and if even one is omitted, the implementation comes to a screeching halt. The screeching seems to always attract the attention of the Chief Executive Officer. The many steps required to install a package can be broken down into four phases: preinstallation, installation, conversion, and postmortem.

PREINSTALLATION PHASE

This phase begins with the decision to purchase a particular package, and ends when the implementation planning is completed. First, an implementation team must be formed of data processing personnel and end users. This team must include the members responsible for the package selection, especially the driving force. The team should also include the data processing technicians who will install and maintain the system as well as the end users who will test it and ultimately use it.

This team should remain together through the entire implementation and conversion. The first official business of the team is to corner a technical representative from the vendor for a one- or two-day session. This time will be considered as training time by the vendor and will be subtracted from the total time allotted for training. Do not quibble over this. This session is absolutely necessary and well worth it.

The session topic will be "How do we use the package in our organization." Hold the session away from telephones and day-to-day business, preferably in a hotel conference room or some other isolated location. Arrange the meeting so that there are no interruptions. Although this requires scheduling and costs money, it is worth it. After all, the future of the company is being planned.

The goal of this meeting is to bridge the gap between what the new package is capable of doing and how the company wants to do business. This gap may be only administrative. For example, the current payroll and personnel systems may be separate and have separate staffs supporting them. If the new package is combined, it must be decided who submits which forms and how security and control are handled.

Undoubtedly other gaps will be found. There may be functions currently performed that the package either does not provide or provides manually. Accrual of benefit hours in personnel/payroll systems provides a classic example. The company may have one set of rules for employees in bargaining units, another for salespeople, and yet another for executives. It can be terribly complicated. The following is typical. "The employees accrue two days in each calendar quarter after the first full calendar quarter of employment. After six months, they are eligible to use the days accrued up to the beginning of the current calendar year, provided. . . . "

These rules are difficult to define even in union contracts, but they vary so widely that it is almost impossible to provide a general solution for them in packages. The package probably will provide a few simple alternatives for accruing hours each payroll cycle, and will expect manual input to set the rates of accrual. There are several questions to be answered. Can the accrual policy be changed to conform to the package? Will accruals be done with manual input? (The staff might rebel at this.) Is a front-end system needed that generates input to the package to accrue benefit data? Must the package be modified to do the proper accruals automatically?

This process of reviewing the unique functions with the technical representative will help tremendously. Everyone will learn a good deal about the way the package works. The technical representative may know other companies that have installed the package and have already solved some of the same problems. The review may also identify potential changes in input and output of data in the package, and so this analysis should be done before reviewing the input and output data.

Developing an Input Strategy

In the system being replaced, there are input forms, policies, and procedures for entering data into the system. With the new package, the vendor will provide sample input forms, but these will be different from the current forms. The few procedures provided may be inconsistent with the organization. The package will not contain policies. In addition, in trying to be all things to all people, packages provide many transactions and forms that either will not be used by some companies or will differ only slightly from other similar forms. How will these forms be used?

The goal of the input strategy session is to rough out a plan for getting data into the system. Take a copy of each current input form to the session. Review these forms with the technical representative and identify the functions they perform, such as changing data, creating new master records, deleting records, and adjusting data. Find out how each of these functions can be accomplished with the package. Some manual functions in the current system may be performed automatically by the new package, so that no input is needed. Other functions may be combined into a single input form in the new system.

Simplify wherever possible. However, sometimes the functions must be performed in separate departments. Then they should not be combined on a single form. Some accounts payable and payroll systems have a single form to both void and record handwritten checks. One simply checks the appropriate box to identify either void or handwritten. Some companies prefer not to use such dual-purpose forms. They use multipart checks so that the check stub itself becomes the input form for the handwritten check. When the check is prepared, the input document is prepared simultaneously and always agrees with the check as written.

The important thing to remember is that the forms the vendor provides are merely templates for various transactions that the package accepts. Someone can cut and paste them to their heart's content as long as the form can be keyed correctly. This means that the order of fields for a transaction can be resequenced on a form, fields deleted, or unnecessary fields left out. Fields might even be shortened, such as an address, city, and name field. None of these changes prevents an operator from keying transactions in the form the package expects. Fields cannot, however, be added (another set of discount terms), lengthened (extend the address from 30 characters to 35), or deleted (if it is a required field). Any of these changes would create a transaction different from that the system expects.

When the group has identified and roughed out all of the forms needed by the package, all that remains is for someone to go over the forms to add logos, signature blocks, and instructions, and clean up the art work. However, the big job is done. An input strategy now exists, and the group members should have a good feeling about how the package works and how it will be used.

Developing an Output Strategy

By now, the group is familiar with the functions the package is to perform and how it is to be fed data. The next step is to determine what the package should produce as output.

Most application packages have three classes of output: standard, optional, and user defined. The standard output is produced automatically as part of the normal execution of the package. This includes edit and control reports, checks, statements, registers, and interface files. Optional reports are those the vendor has programmed in some generic way, but whether they are produced is left up to each installation. The third set of output constitutes most of the volume. It must be defined completely by each installation. Reports must be formatted, their content determined, and their run schedule planned. User-defined output usually is produced by a report writer.

Copies of all the reports and file layouts that are currently used should be available at the meeting, along with samples of the new output needed. Review these against the standard and optional output of the package to determine how to use them and what additional output must be created with the report writer. Determine whether all the reports are needed, eliminating when possible. With a report writer, it is fairly easy to add new reports. Basic human nature makes it difficult to kill an unused report once it is implemented. The time to do this is while installing a new system—now.

Have the technical representative determine which of the reports and output files that must be added to the package can be produced by the report writer. Many report formats are ideal for report writers, some are awkward, and a few are impossible.

With a little compromise, there may be a way to accept what the report writer produces. For example, most report writers cannot recap subtotals at the end of a report. But by splitting the report into two parts, a detail and a summary, the summary report can be made to serve as a recap of the totals. If such compromises can be accepted, the implementation will go much more smoothly.

If there are still reports and files that cannot be handled by the package, they must be programmed. Find out which ones they are as soon as possible because the programming will be excruciatingly slow.

Developing a Test Plan

The package must be tested before it is implemented. It will not need unit testing, which is the testing of individual programs, except for those programs modified or added to the package. It will, however, need system testing. System testing involves testing the package as a whole. The following steps are used in testing the system.

Develop the Test Plan

Systems testing should not be thought of as an isolated event that is done once and then forgotten. It should be done as an inherent part of the system and set up so that it can be done throughout the life of the system. The first requirement of maintenance is a means of system testing. Viewed this way, the system test is something that must be maintained. It is also something that requires planning—not just planning what to test, but also planning on how the testing can be done once the system is in production. The things to consider are:

1. The test data, usually transactions. Both good and bad transactions are needed to test the system. The transactions should be maintained and added to during the life of the package so that when maintenance changes occur, someone can test that old errors are not reintroduced.
2. The methods of generating test data. It may be possible to do this by hand, to do this by converting old transactions, or to do this by generating the data with a program, perhaps by sampling a file.
3. The master files for testing. Programs may have to be written to convert old master files to be used by the new package. Programs usually are needed to load the master files and to back them up if they are updated or undergo maintenance.
4. The plan for testing during production. The maintenance of test master files, calendars, the changing content of actual master files, the method of loading test files, and the test JCL need to be considered.

Write the Utility and File Dump Programs Necessary

In addition to testing, programs are needed to produce formatted dumps of master and transaction files. Write a file dump program for each master file, and make the dump program an inherent part of the system. The same program usually can be written to load, copy, dump, and, if necessary, have code inserted to change a specific field in a specific transaction (as is sometimes necessary during maintenance).

Establish the Criteria for Accepting the Package into Production

Testing is not static, even with a test plan. The testing requirements will grow and change with the testing. Ultimately a decision must be made whether the package is ready to begin production. The criteria for this should be a part of the plan.

Revise the Manual Procedures

The final part of system testing is to iron out any problems in the manual procedures. This may necessitate updating the user's manual.

Developing a Conversion Strategy

While the actual conversion takes place at the end of implementation, it should be one of the first things planned. Discuss it in the meeting with the technical representative.

There are several approaches to implementing a package. The ideal way is to implement the package during the system test. This can be done for an entirely new application in which no conversion is required. Real data are fed into the package for testing, and when the system is accepted, production has already begun.

Unfortunately, there is usually an existing system to be replaced. The main choices are a swift, clean cutover, stopping the old system and starting the new, or to run both the old and new systems in parallel until the new package is proved. The advantage of the clean cutover is that it is less work. The disadvantage is that it is high risk. The advantages and disadvantages of running in parallel are the exact opposite.

There are also variations in implementing systems. The end users can fill out duplicate input forms for the old and new systems for parallel running, the old transactions can be converted into the new format for parallel running, and master files can be converted back and forth.

Another way to implement a package is in phases. The main part of the package is implemented first, and then new features are added along the way so that the implementation team does not become swamped with too much at once.

A company often does not have full freedom of choice in the way it implements. It may be constrained by the schedule or what is feasible. End users may balk at filling out duplicate input forms. It is almost impossible to run an on-line system in parallel. There is more flexibility with a batch system that is run periodically.

However the package is implemented, it must never be placed in production without testing it with real data and having a fallback position if things go wrong. Made up data, such as those created for the system testing, can never anticipate all the strange and unusual situations that occur with real data.

In implementing a new package driven by transactions, there is often an option of converting the master files directly with a file-to-file conversion, or of converting the old master file records into transactions to be fed into the new package. The latter is preferable because the new transactions can be edited as they go into the package, which can catch not only data errors but also conversion errors. The natural temptation is to attempt a file-to-file conversion. Do not try it. Package system master files are so complex that there is never enough information when the package is first received to properly do the job. Even after two years of using the package, programmers may not know enough to do it. (They would, however, know enough not to try it.)

The main problem with file-to-file conversions is the lack of control and file integrity. Good audit controls are missing. If the conversion should inadvertently overlook a field, the potential errors may not occur for months or even years. The transactions could, of course, be entered manually, but if the data are in machine-readable form, a program should be written to convert it into the proper format.

There is more to the strategy than just choosing between a file-to-file, manual, or file-transaction-file conversion. The new package will have more fields of information than in the old system. The method of handling these additional fields must be decided. The choices are usually to accept default values or enter manual transactions. The plan should also determine which files must be converted and when the conversion should be done.

Developing the Implementation Work Plan

The technical representative can help put together an implementation work plan. This plan lists all the tasks that need to be done, the critical paths, and the estimated time required for each. At the very least, the plan should include the tasks listed in this chapter.

After the meeting is over, the implementation can begin.

IMPLEMENTATION PHASE

This phase represents the bulk of the work in installing a package. There is a host of tasks, some specific to each organization, but many that apply to everyone. They are discussed next. There is nothing magical about the order. Some tasks may run concurrently or precede or follow each other. Only by knowing an organization can the order be decided.

Training

The amount of training required varies with the package, but it should not be overlooked. Not only do people need to be trained, but they also need training materials, people to train them, and time in which to train. Training is needed for data processing, end users, and operations. One of the big advantages of doing the user's manual early is that it is then available when the end users need it for training. In fact, implementation is the time that the user's manual is most needed.

The vendor usually offers on-site training. Some of this training has already been used for the first meeting with the technical representative. The vendor probably has already set aside the training time for the end users and data processing. However, it is the company's time and it should use the time as necessary.

The vendor should train only the members of the implementation group. If there is additional corporate-wide training to do, the group should provide it. The vendor's people should not be turned loose on an organization. Tempting as it may be to use their knowledge and training skills to train all of the other personnel, there are two problems. First, the system they teach is different from the system that will be run at any company. Only people within a company can teach the company's system. Second, teaching is learning. As people in the company prepare to teach others, they will learn more about the package themselves.

Divide the training time into two sections: user training, which trains people on how to use the system, and data processing training, which trains people on how to install the package programs. Both data processing and the end users should attend the user training. The data processing training will be so technical that it is unlikely to be of interest to end users.

Documentation

One problem with vendor documentation is that there is so much of it. It is a job just to find one's way through it. A good portion of the documentation covers technical data processing issues, such as file and record layouts and program narratives. The balance of the documentation describes system functions from an end-user point of view.

Unfortunately, as good as the end-user documentation may be, it usually cannot be used directly. It is missing a vital ingredient—corporate policy. Chances are, the company will already have its own input forms and reports as well.

The writing of the company's own user manual should start as soon as the first meeting with the technical representative is over. Rough drafts of the input forms and reports have already been prepared, and these can be used to form the basis of the user manual. The manual should describe each input form and how it is used. Include a sample of each output report and describe each column or field on it. The manual should include corporate policy in such a way that it appears indivisible from the package's function.

The description of how to use the package will comprise most of the manual. Here is where corporate policy is specified. Provide a description of each of the actions a user will need to take. For example, an accounts payable system needs descriptions on how to add vendors, pay invoices, void checks, and input handwritten checks. For a payroll system, instructions are needed for adding employees, making pay increases, terminating employees, entering time cards and handwritten checks, and voiding checks. Each description should show a sample form filled out correctly.

All packages need a detailed description of how to balance input transactions and verify the controls. This is critical because it determines the integrity of the system.

Add to the manual a set of appendices that contain reference information and tables. These tables should list all special codes used in the package, such as vendor types, job codes, and account numbers. The reference information might include a list of postal abbreviation codes and tax formulas or tables.

Finish the first draft of the manual and distribute it before the end of system testing. Let the end users review the manual and criticize it.

They may find holes in the controls or even in the system, and they most certainly will find holes in the documentation. This is the best time to validate documentation—when the package is new and unknown. Every flaw is apparent as an open window on a snowy, stormy day. Publish a corrected draft in time for the parallel run of the package.

Installing the System

Besides the manuals, the vendor will send a magnetic tape containing the system. This tape will contain the COBOL source statements for the programs, the object programs (the compiled source programs), sample job control, and probably test data.

Early on, data processing has an important decision to make regarding how the source code will be handled within the data center. Typically, the vendors take one of two approaches. Either they write their own source statement maintenance program to store, recall, and update source programs, or they use one of the IBM utility programs, such as IEBUPDTE under OS and MAINT under DOS.

Either of these methods will work in an installation, but both are crude, batch-oriented approaches. If an installation uses a more sophisticated source library system, such as Librarian or Panvalet, or if it uses on-line program development tools, it will want to use these instead of what the vendor provides. There are two problems to solve: How is the vendor's tape unloaded into the system? How are future vendor maintenance changes applied? Updates may arrive on card or tape, but they must be applied to the original source programs. Any solution must be ongoing because it will be used again and again.

Object Code and Compilation

Many vendors supply object code with their packages. This lets the package be quickly installed without compiling programs. However, each program should be compiled immediately. This is important for several reasons. First, it verifies that the source programs are all present, complete, and correct. Second, compilation and cross-reference listings are needed for each of the programs. Third, the object programs the vendor provides are usually compiled in as neutral an environment as possible (IBM 360) so that they do not necessarily take advantage of the instruction sets on the more modern equipment.

Operational Strategy

While the operational strategy planning may begin during the preinstallation phase, it is better to wait until the data processing personnel
have received their technical training and the programs have been
compiled. Hold an operational strategy meeting that includes the end
users, programmers, system analysts, operations managers, data control supervisors, and quality assurance. When operations and data control personnel are left out of strategy meetings—as they frequently
are—bad things usually result.

The purpose of this meeting is to determine how the system will be
run in production. The vendors will, of course, provide a system flow
chart and sample JCL, but the operational flow will have to be reconstructed to be consistent with the installation's standards. The meeting should determine specifics: How many edit cycles will be run?
Will the edit be a separate job stream from the update? Should generation data groups be used? How many generations should be kept? Are
the files disk or tape? Should printed output be backed up to tape?
When do the various phases of the system run? What is the turnaround
schedule? How are errors corrected? Who has control over negotiable
computer forms like check stock?

The data processing technicians should conduct this meeting because they know the most about the internals of the package. The end
users and the operations group should have the final say about the
way the package is run. They are ultimately the ones most affected by
it.

The data processing technicians should have in hand the file size
estimates, run time estimates, and a large systems flow chart. The
products of the meeting should be a new systems flow chart with individual job streams designated, disk and tape requirements, production schedules, and a definition of the data control process.

Job Control Language

The vendor-supplied JCL must be broken up into the job streams defined in the operational strategy meeting. It must also be modified to
have the proper disk and tape assignments and conform to the in-
house data set naming conventions and other data processing standards. As received from the vendors, it represents only a good skeleton with which to begin working to create the production JCL.

Program Modifications

Try as one may, the package probably cannot be used without modification. Though everyone wants to run a "vanilla" version of the package, even the vendors themselves recognize that this is not likely and they make accommodations accordingly. Most package systems have designated user exits or calls to user-supplied subroutines to accommodate special editing, special calculations, or any other unique processing.

User exits are designated ranges of line numbers located at strategic processing points in the package programs. Typically, the vendors promise to hold these line numbers inviolate. That is, they will not provide any program updates that would wipe out these areas. In addition, the vendors provide documentation about the status of working storage and file buffers at each of these points.

Calls to user subroutines are handled a little differently. The vendors usually place these subroutine calls at the same strategic processing points that user exits would be located. However, because the calls are active, the vendors may supply dummy subroutines that merely return control to the main program without doing anything. To install modifications, subprograms are written, compiled, and linked to the main program in place of the vendor-supplied dummy routines.

Changes to the package should utilize the user exits or subroutine calls provided if at all possible. Anything else is dangerous and probably invalidates the warranty. When planning a user exit or subroutine, remember the following:

1. Double and triple check that the function being added is not provided by the package, albeit in some esoteric or awkward fashion. Even after using a package for a year, people will be aware of only two thirds of its capabilities. These big, complex systems cannot be swallowed at one or two sittings.

2. Before making the modifications, call the vendor's technical representative and ask if the function can be provided some other way within the package. There may be an easy answer. Keep an open mind. Their solution may not be exactly what is wanted, but if it is close without requiring a modification, go for it. At least it provides an interim solution. If a modification is required, the vendor will say so, after trying several alternatives first. The vendor may also point out the easiest way to

make the modifications. If another company has already done something similar, the vendor may know about it.

3. Make any changes consistent with the package concept. Keep data names consistent with those used by the vendor. In trying to stay consistent with the package concept, avoid limiting any of the capabilities of the package. For example, a payroll package may handle weekly, biweekly, semimonthy, and monthly payroll. Even if the package is to be used with only a biweekly pay cycle, do not hard-wire an 80-hour period into an accrual routine. Handle it generically like the vendor does: look at the pay frequency indicator to determine the hours in the pay period.

4. Parameterize where possible. If a special Long Term Disability (LTD) deduction calculation must be installed in a payroll package, parameterize it. Put the constants and factors in the formula into a table in a file. This way when the per thousand rate goes from $1.15 to $1.27 next year, it is simply a matter of entering a transaction to change the rate, not a programming change.

5. Save the changes separately. Once the changes have been incorporated into the package, the result will be a complete set of new programs. This is great, but what if the vendor sends out a new copy of a program instead of just updates to it? How are the customization changes reapplied? The best way is to keep a separate copy of the them.

Testing

Testing consists of system testing, much of which is done in the form of parallel runs. System testing is done in order to uncover interface problems, volume problems, performance problems, and design problems. It involves testing the system as a whole rather than as individual components. System testing can also overlap conversion. Conversion, especially file and transaction conversions, may be necessary to generate test data for system testing.

The data from even two or three run cycles often are not adequate to shake out some problems. Year-end closing and file conversion for a new year always result in special problems.

Problems uncovered during system testing must be solved. This may entail debugging, introducing changes to resolve performance problems, or revising the specifications because of interface problems.

System testing is the most important step in the entire schedule. Most projects stay on schedule until the system testing begins. Problems discovered here may affect many programs and may even affect the design of the system. The sooner these can be identified, the better it will be for everyone.

Probably the biggest waste of effort in a data center is in fighting brushfires and tracking down errors. Oddly enough, few data centers make the effort to create and maintain adequate test data. Every time a change or enhancement is installed, new test data are prepared, and perhaps a parallel run is made, but there is still a good chance the package will fail when run live. Test data should be treated as an integral part of the package. They should contain:

1. Transactions that test all the features used in the package, especially those added with user exits.
2. Transactions that test all of the editing in the system, including range checks, numeric checks, and validations.
3. Transactions that have failed in the past. If a transaction once blew up the system or did not process properly, include it in the test data. Nothing is more frustrating than having a problem reappear after it supposedly has been fixed.
4. Special processing. Be sure the test data include not only normal cycle processing, but also any month-end, quarter-end, or year-end processing as well. This may necessitate setting up more than one set of test data.

Test data are dynamic. Let both junior data processing people and end users add data. The volume will not hurt. The users should be made familiar with the test data. They should participate in developing test plans for the package. This way they will have some measure of confidence that the package will work when implemented.

The test data will consist of master files, transaction files, tables, copies of the resulting output reports, and file dumps. The vendor's test data may be a start for developing the test data, but remember that it is far from being complete.

Parallel Runs

The last part of system testing is to run the new package in parallel with the old system. Parallel runs are difficult, but they make great tests. They are especially hard on end users, who must do most of the work. There is one aspect of parallel runs that is very appealing. Since the old system is still running, the parallel run need not actually be performed at the same time. It could occur weeks or even months later. It can also be run and rerun as errors are corrected.

The parallel run tests the conversion programs at the same time as everything else. For a payroll system, there may be a week between cycles. With an accounts payable system, there are probably a few days before the next cycle. An on-line accounts receivable system may have only overnight.

Systems usually do not parallel exactly. Wherever values are calculated rather than entered, the results may vary from system to system. This particularly true of payroll. In payroll, there may be penny rounding differences for wages and deductions. Often, too, the tax calculation methods will vary. A 10-cent variation per person on gross and net pay may be as close as one can get for a payroll system. Fixed assests and general ledger, because of allocations, are also likely to have penny rounding errors. Accounts payable and accounts receivable are more likely to compare exactly.

CONVERSION

After all programs are installed and tested and the package is run in parallel, it is time to convert. If parallel runs have been made, the conversion programs are probably well tested. If not, some means must be devised to test the results of conversion. Usually there are some representative reports that can be run for a system to verify accuracy and balances. Registers, trial balances, and file dumps are also good.

Practice the procedures and timing when running conversions for the parallel runs. Usually the timing for a live conversion is tight and it must work the first time. One last thing to do in the conversion— make sure that no one on the conversion team leaves town.

POSTMORTEM

Once conversion is over and the system has run a few cycles and everyone has received the waves of congratulations (or slings and arrows of outrage), hold a postmortem with all members of the implementation team and the end users. This eases tension and redirects the effort into turning the infant system into a well-maintained adult. The purpose is to record both what went right and what went wrong. Note any future changes that people feel should be made to the system. The changes can be made maintenance tasks.

The postmortem forces people to review the system and distill what they have learned from implementing it. The postmortem should include the project history, how well schedules were met, and cost. Data processing people especially need to build up their own data base of costing and estimating information. Many attempts have been made to formalize both, but ultimately it comes down to the judgment and experience of the individual person. Make sure the people retain their experience.

Chapter 19
Living With a Package

Once it is implemented, a package will be around for several years. It will need care and feeding if it is to flourish.

USING THE SYTEM

An immediate problem after completing a system is to get people to use it. If a system represents a new way of doing business, some people will not understand this and will continue operating as they did under the old system. They must be made to accept the changes. It takes a combination of motivation, training, and coercion to make this occur. Above all, it needs a driving force.

MAINTENANCE AND ENHANCEMENTS

In all likelihood, while the struggle is still going on to implement the package, the vendor will be sending out updates, corrections, and possibly even a new version of the package. Chances are, some of these will be received even before the programs are unloaded from the source tape and compiled. This is especially true of payroll packages where tax changes occur constantly. Let us first look at how the vendors supply the program updates and then discuss what should be done with the updates.

How Vendors Supply Maintenance

Vendors usually provide three types of maintenance: unscheduled program fixes, scheduled maintenance, and scheduled new releases.

Unscheduled program fixes are the result of program bugs discovered by the vendor, or, more likely, by another package customer. Usually these changes are quick fixes sent out by the vendor on mimeographed coding sheets or on 80-column punched cards.

Scheduled maintenance includes quarterly, annual, or any other regularly scheduled changes that the vendor must supply. These include annual tax changes, new 1099 forms, and new W-2 formats. These are not quick fixes but are more substantial changes. They are usually sent out on minireel tapes or on punched cards.

Many vendors schedule regular releases of their packages. This is particularly true of those who continually develop and enhance their products. Perhaps part of the reason for the new releases is that the promise of a new release on the horizon is an effective marketing tool. Whatever the customer wants is bound to be in the new release.

There is some abuse of the term "release" among the vendors, but it is usually reserved for significant enhancements to their products. These changes may include a major new feature, such as budgeting for general ledger, or a change in the structure of the files or programs.

Most vendors incorporate all the interim maintenance, both scheduled and unscheduled, provided since the last release, into the latest release. Thus if all the maintenance has not been applied, it will not matter after the latest release is installed. If there are material changes to files, the vendor will provide a conversion program to convert existing files from the old format to the new.

Handling Vendor Maintenance

There are a number of things to consider in applying vendor maintenance. First, if the package is still being installed, delay applying any of the updates until after the package is in production. The exception is if the implementation uncovers bugs or if enough time passes so that required changes, such as for taxes, must be applied. Similarly, if a new release is scheduled around the time the package is being tested and installed, delay the testing and implementation until after the new release is received. It is very confusing trying to test and learn a new system while it is being changed—the classic case of trying to hit a moving target.

Generally, it is a good idea to age any vendor-supplied maintenance or new releases. Typically, these updates have many more flaws than the original product. If a change is needed to solve a critical problem, then do it; otherwise let someone else take the risk, trouble, and frustration.

Be sure that one person is designated to receive all maintenance from the vendor. This person should evaluate each update as it arrives, and qualify it as critical (requiring immediate application), desirable (scheduled as a maintenance task), or unnecessary (to be applied as time allows or ignored until the next release). A mistake that many companies make is to assume that a package requires no effort once it is implemented. Effort is required, and it must be budgeted.

SYSTEM WEARING OUT

All systems, even package systems, eventually wear out. Because a package system is maintained and enhanced by a vendor for a community of users, it has a very long potential life. However, the success of a package system depends on how well it meets the needs of the application, and these needs are not static. If the needs change sufficiently, the package may no longer fit. It has, in fact, worn out.

When a package wears out, the company is left in the same position it was when it began the selection. Someone must do a requirements analysis, write an RFP, select a new package, and implement it. The exact same thing can happen when the wrong package is selected— one that does not fit. The only recourse may be to go through the selection process again. (Usually a new group of people select the next package—there is a lot of job changing when a package fails.)

All in all, living with a package is the best part. Once the selection and implementation of a package are completed, living with it is downright enjoyable.

Chapter 20
Special Problems

In this chapter we examine a few of the special problems one may encounter in selecting and implementing package systems. These are only the general problems—every package implementation has unique problems as well.

NON-IBM COMPUTERS

IBM's 360/370/43xx/30xx hardware and OS and DOS software have become the de facto standards for large computer systems. The most popular financial packages will all run on IBM's large computers. What if the computer is not IBM compatable? The market is considerably smaller for financial packages on non-IBM computers. Although several of the vendors do modify their packages to run on non-IBM computers, this helps only if converted for your non-IBM computer.

With a non-IBM computer, there are three possibilities for software packages. First, a vendor may market a package especially for a computer. The vendor would be carving out a unique portion of the market where there probably would be little competition. If a vendor has a package especially for the computer, the problem is the same as if it were an IBM computer—is there a match?

However, rarely is a financial package just for a large non-IBM computer. There may be several specialized packages, but there will be few generalized financial systems.

This brings up the second possibility. A vendor may market a non-IBM version of an IBM package. This too can work well, but it has several problems. The IBM package will be first string, and the non-IBM package will be second string. The IBM package will get more attention, the documentation will be geared to IBM, the operating system interfaces will be designed for IBM computers, and most of the support people will know IBM. The IBM version of the financial package is also likely to be a version ahead of the non-IBM versions. Changes and enchancements will come to the IBM verison first, and then trickle down to the non-IBM version. The non-IBM versions will not be as thoroughly tested, and there will be more shortcuts taken in the non-IBM version than the IBM.

Look at the problems from the vendor's point of view. One computer system, the IBM compatible, constitutes about 70% of the large-computer market. There are about eight other vendors that share the remaining 30%. Trying to get adequate computer time and trying to hire people experienced on the eight other computers is an overwhelming problem that can be solved only with a lot of unhappy compromises.

The final possibility is that the vendor does not have a version of the package converted to a non-IBM computer. Some salespeople, if hungry enough, will argue that because this package is written in a high-level, machine-independent language such as COBOL, the conversion is easy. Just the oppostie is true. COBOL, for example, has many language statements that specify hardware and are hardware dependent. Even with an ANS standard for COBOL, compilers differ remarkably among different computers. The operating sytems also differ. If the IBM package uses the ISAM or VSAM access method and it is not supported on a non-IBM computer's operating system or COBOL compiler, the conversion problems would be enormous. Even if it is supported, there may be subtle differences waiting to sabotage the system.

A company should consider very carefully whether to purchase a package system that has not been implemented on its computer. It will take perhaps half a year to do the conversion, and will cost at least as much as the purchase cost of the package. The cost could also turn out to be much more, and even then the conversion might be unsuccessful.

To get some perspective of the cost, consider one company that specializes in conversions using many automated conversion tools. This company charged $0.80 per source statement as of 1980 to convert from one version of COBOL to another. Thus a 50,000-statement program would cost $40,000 to convert. This high cost is a realistic cost today.

Even if the package is successfully converted to an non-IBM computer, there is the problem of keeping up with the changes and enhancements supplied by the vendor. Usually the converted version of the package ends up frozen, which loses one of the major advantages of a package system. Then too, vendors are reluctant to warranty converted systems.

Sometimes vendors will underwrite part of the conversion cost in exchange for rights to the converted version. The vendor then offers this as the non-IBM version. This reduces costs, but that is about all. The package will still end up being a frozen version because the vendor has no way of updating it. Since this is the way many non-IBM versions of systems come into being, it also explains why the quality is often suspect.

EXTENSIVE MODIFICATIONS TO A PACKAGE

Making extensive modifications to a package brings two problems. First, it makes the package cost much more and takes longer to implement. Second, it may make it impossible to apply the vendor's maintenance and enchancements. What happens is that two major advantages of a package are lost: its lower cost and the maintenance and enhancements.

Unfortunately, major changes generally arrive incrementally, and so it is not clear at the beginning that the changes will be major. They often begin small and then grow, sometimes taking over the entire implementation. Since half of a package's cost is up front and cannot be recovered once it is purchased, it is extremely difficult to make the decision later that the modifications are too major to be done.

If one can determine that major changes are required before selecting the package, there is an opportunity to evalutate them and their effect before committing to the package. If the package is bought before it is found out that major changes are required, the choice is the difficult one of discarding the package or trying to implement the changes.

Although a package in which major changes must be made may still cost less than developing a system internally, it brings other problems. Maintenance is difficult because changes by the vendor may affect the modifications made to the package. Even more serious is the morale problem that changes cause. Programmers can get enthusiastic about developing a system, but making major changes to a package is not likely to excite anyone. It may be easier to write the entire system within the company than it would be to try to modify a package system if the changes are truly major.

The serious consequences of having to make major changes to a package point out the need to make the correct selection.

IMPLEMENTING CHANGE THROUGH A PACKAGE

There is a syndrome that often occurs in selecting a package that goes like this: "Our people are all fouled up and don't know what they are doing. Let's get a package in here and force the people to conform to it. After all, the package vendors are the real experts and know how their type of application should be run."

This view has resulted in some rare successes but more frequent failures. Software vendors have no way of knowing how someone should run their business. A few of them do not run their own businesses too well. They can get a fairly good feel of how a group of users want to run their businesses. Remember, though, even if the package is installed at 500 companies, all 500 may be totally different from your company.

There is another problem in letting the package be the agent of change. Packages can be defeated. They are so difficult to implement that they are relatively easy to defeat. When an attempt is made to force people to accept a package, either the package or the people will go. There are times a package can be successfully forced onto reluctant users to effect change. When the forcing is done by someone very high up in the company, it can work. Not only can higher-ups force change, but they are likely to know what they want.

When it is data processing that is doing the forcing, failure is almost certain. First, data processing probably does not really know what is needed. Second, data processing does not have the authority to force people to change. But a forceful high executive can do wonders in effecting change.

VENDOR DISCONTINUES SUPPORT

In the vendor selection, it is difficult to predict which vendors will be in business a few years from now. At various times, Rolls-Royce, Penn Central, Lockheed, Chrysler, Pan-American, New York City and Cleveland have courted bankruptcy. If these can fail, what cannot?

What does a company do if the vendor goes out of business or is forced to drop its support? Nothing happens immediately. Things go on just as they have, except vendor maintenance is no longer received and no one answers the vendor's hot line. As time goes on, this becomes more and more of a problem, but it may take a few months. There is time to prepare.

The company should always have a copy of the source listing and the source programs. This allows error corrections and even enhancements to be made. But more important, it is absolutely necessary to keep the package running even with no changes. As the computer goes from one operating system version to another, there always seems to be some glitch that requires a program to be recompiled. If there is no source to recompile, there is trouble.

If a vendor of a popular package goes out of business, it is almost certain that either another company will take over the package or a small software company will spring up to take over maintenance and perhaps even add enhancements.

In short, it is inconvenient if a vendor goes out of business. It is not a disaster if the package continues to be maintained. If the package is not maintained, start looking for another one.

PACKAGE NOT FULLY IMPLEMENTED

A slightly different problem arises when only a portion of the company is converted to a new package. At the end of conversion, people are so exhausted and unenthusiastic that it is difficult to complete the remainder of the company. In a multicompany corporation, a new personnel/payroll package may be implemented for the main company, but implementing it for the subsidiaries may be deferred. This too can be a good and perhaps necessary part of the conversion plan.

Implementing the package for the remainder of the corporation cannot be done as a data processing maintenance task. It is too big and requires too much user involvement. There is only one way to complete the implementation, and that is to do it the same way that the job was begun. The implementation team has some things in its favor. Having already implemented the package for a portion of the company, they know what must be done and some of the problems they will encounter. This is an advantage they did not have when they began. But the more delay, the more they lose this advantage.

For this reason, the implementation of the package for the remainder of the company will be much easier than the initial implementation if it is done soon. It will still be difficult, but nothing like what it was. The main problems will be people rather than technical ones. The plan to complete the implementation should be simple. Push as hard and as fast as possible to finish the job. The more delay, the more difficult it becomes because people start to lose the knowledge they have gained, and some of the people who did the original implementation may leave the company.

Even after a full implementation, the vendor will add enhancements, so that "implementation" is constant. Someone should keep in touch with the vendor and keep active in user groups, both to be aware of what the vendor is doing and also to benefit from the experience of other users of the package.

Chapter 21
How to Learn
a System

There are several techniques one can use to learn a system, whether one is an end user or in data processing. This chapter describes these techniques for the person who must learn the details of a package. The chapter makes the assumption that the reader is the unfortunate person who is charged with learning the system.

READING THE DOCUMENTATION

There are drier things to read than documentation of a system, but they do not come readily to mind. In an ideal society, reading computer documentation would perhaps be incorporated into the criminal justice system, standing somewhere between a jail sentence and capital punishment.

The problem is compounded by the vendors, who, aware that documentation is always a problem in data processing, try to bury the user in it. They act as if the scale upon which documentation is measured is a produce scale. The more it weighs, the better it is. How does one approach documentation that—for a single system—can occupy three feet of shelf space? Well, it is best not to do it on a full stomach after a three-martini lunch.

Never begin by reading the documentation straight through. There is too much. A package will have a user's manual, a programmer's or systems manual, a report writer manual, and perhaps an operations manual. There may be more. The first step is to decide what to read. If no custom reports are generated, there is little need to read the report writer manual. End users can probably get by with skimming the programmer's manual to familiarize themselves with what it contains. (Even end users may need to refer to the programmer's manual for questions because it contains the most detail.)

The first problem is to obtain copies of the appropriate manuals.

Each person should have his or her own copies, even if this means buying extra copies from the vendor.

The starting place for both end users and programmers is the user's manual. It is more readable than the other documentation. The user's manual tells what the system is intended to do, which lets one learn a great deal about the sytem by implication and inference. Although the user's manual will be organized to be read from beginning to end, do not be afraid to skip around. There is no need to become familiar with features that will not be used. It is all right to flip back and forth in the manual. It is less important to know everything in the manual than to know what is in the manual and how to locate it.

It is extremely difficult to open a manual and begin reading it. People find themselves skimming over the words without absorbing them. An entire page or section can be read without instilling the ability to recall anything that was discussed. A person must develop some method to make the reading interesting.

Use the RFP as a guide in reading the manual, and check off things on the RFP as the manual describes how they are done. This helps direct the reading and gives an incentive to read. Without such an incentive, it is difficult to struggle through a manual. Also, checking off the items on the RFP helps keep track of the progress. It forces the reader to really understand how she or he is going to implement the RFP features with the package. Keep in mind that the manual is not read to see if the features are in the package but to see how to implement features by using the package.

OUTSIDE HELP

The easiest way to learn a package is to have someone else do it and then brief whoever must learn it. This saves time and is much more concise. As a variation on this, one might consider hiring a consultant who has already implemented the package. Having gone through one implementation, the consultant will know the package and be aware of many of the problem areas. The package is learned from the consultant, at least initially.

WRITE A MANUAL

Perhaps the best way to learn a system is to write a manual for it. A user's manual will have to be written for the package anyway. (Even if a user's manual is provided by the vendor, it will be too general.) An installation's user manual will reflect company policies, procedures, and forms. Since this manual must be written even for a packaged system, one can combine this with learning the system. There is nothing better to make a person learn something than to have to write a manual for it—except to give classes in it. And so a person might also want to organize some classes in the new system, and teaching them too will ensure that at least this person learns the system.

PLAN THE MODIFICATIONS

As people begin learning the system they probably already know some modifications that must be made. During the implementation, more will be discovered. Learning what modifications must be made and researching ways to make the modifications is another way of learning the system. The more directed people are in using the documentation, the faster they learn, the more they can concentrate, and the more interesting it is.

ANSWERING QUESTIONS

Another method of focusing attention in reading is to form a list of questions that must be answered. Everyone on the project will have a large number of questions. Get these written down and study the documentation with an eye toward answering them. More questions continually crop up, and they should be noted and answered too. When the questions have been answered, they probably have generated understanding of the documentation.

One of the things that takes a considerable amount of time in implementing a package, although perhaps it is not actually a part of implementation, is answering questions. There is a constant barrage of "What if," "Can we do this," "What happens if we do this" type of questions. Usually answering these questions takes quite a bit of time because they must be researched. And even after several hours of poring through documentation, the answer might be something like "I think so, but we'll have to try it."

One way to solve this problem is to set up a dummy corporation. Most financial packages provide for separate corporate entities. Set up a dummy corporation and then make changes or enter test data against this dummy corporation. When a question arises about the effect of a transaction, enter the transaction against the dummy corporation and see what happens. The dummy corporation lets the package be tested without the overhead of having to load separate test files. The dummy corporation is set up as a part of the normal system to allow testing at any time. Often it is quicker and less expensive to try something than it is to attempt to discover the answer by reading the documentation.

Chapter 22
Application Generators

Throughout this book, we have tried to hammer home three points:

1. There is no make-versus-buy decision for computer systems. A company should buy if it can; otherwise it should make.
2. Installing a package is the process of trying to make something fit that does not necessarily fit.
3. The process must have a driving force.

What can a company do if it cannot buy a package that is even close to what it needs and there is no time to design, code, and implement a system? An application generator may be the answer. Application generators are fairly new tools. The authors had firsthand experience with one in the mid-1970s and found it to be a very exciting alternative to programming.

BASIC CONCEPT

The basic idea behind the application generator is to isolate the difficult aspects of financial applications, such as batching, posting, editing, reporting, sorting, summarizing, and table handling. Application generators provide a shell into which the user puts parameters that tell what is to be done. Application generators parameterize practically everything, from input and output file definitions, to batch control, to transaction edit rules, to reports. Application generators bear somewhat the same relationship to COBOL that COBOL does to assembler language.

In a sense, the larger, more flexible financial packages have already made steps in this direction. Many offer user-defined fields and edits, and most offer report writers in lieu of standard report programs. Much of what would be hard-wired or preprogrammed in an in-house system is specified by transactions fed into a package system. Application generators take this process a step further to parameterize many of the functions described in this book.

There are several application generators, with more in development. They all share a similar structure. The heart of these systems is a table- or rule-driven editor. This editor accepts input files in practically any format, batches and edits transactions according to user-provided criteria, does table lookup as necessary to infer needed information, and then generates an output file defined by the user. The input and output file definitions are dictionaries similar to those in data base applications. These dictionaries define the position, length, and format of data within the file records. They also provide a name by which the data are accessed throughout the rest of the system.

Besides maintaining input and output files, the editor can update a set of tables that form a data base of parameters and codes for the system. These tables contain data for validating account numbers, employee numbers, product numbers, and anything else. The tables are defined by dictionaries in the same way as input and output files.

What this means is that all of the frustrating details that are hardwired into packages are put under the direct control of the user. If the CFO reorganizes the company to add another level in the organizational hierarchy, a programmer need only change the input and output dictionaries, reformat the existing files, and load in the new hierarchy of organizations in a table. The only aspects of the system that need change are those which are directly affected by a new level of hierarchy, such as the number of levels of totals in reports. If a field size needs to be expanded to handle a larger name, it is an order of magnitude easier than it would be with a package or an in-house developed system.

Why are application generators not used more frequently? There are several reasons, some good and some bad. We, the authors, can relate our firsthand experience. We were initially opposed to an application generator. We argued with logic, with facts and figures, and with eloquence against the application generator. The company went ahead with it and, sadly enough, we saw all of our arguments proved wrong. Here are some of the reasons that we used to argue against the application generator.

It requires more effort to generate a system than to install a package. This is true, but it misses the point. One would rarely need to use an application generator if there were an application package available that does the job. The time to consider an application generator is when no package fits.

Application generators are not well known or well established.

They may sound great, but will they work? They are expensive, and after spending the money, the application must still be written. These reasons are, of course, specious. They are used to hide the real reason—data processing people are reluctant to accept them.

Data processing people are almost as suspicious and frightened by application generators as they were by COBOL when it first began to replace assembler language. In defense of the data processing people, a large part of the acceptance of COBOL was due to its being a relatively machine-independent language supported by many vendors. An ANS standard was quickly developed for it. With an application generator, one must trust individual software vendors.

Some of data processing's reservations stem from job insecurity. They may not admit it, but tools like application generators that let programmers do in days what it takes months to do in COBOL do not bode well for the full employment of COBOL programmers. In practice, it may just open the floodgates to more applications so that the increase in demand for them exceeds the productivity gains. More programmers will be needed. Unfortunately, data processing people may not see it this way. Also, an expert in an application generator is not as much in demand as a good COBOL programmer, and programmers are sensitive about what looks good on a résumé.

Application generators are less efficient than custom-written programs. The authors argued very strongly against the application generator because a system written in COBOL might have run at least 30% more efficiently. Events made this increase in efficiency irrelevant. By the time a COBOL system could have been written, a new generation of computer hardware effectively increased the efficiency by 1000%.

Data processing people are very concerned with machine efficiency, even though hardware performance/cost ratios are improving and the software development/cost ratios are not. In 1964 it was worth an hour of programmer time to save 2.5 million computer instructions. Today 2.5 million instructions is worth only 7 minutes of a programmer's time.

Data processing people dislike application generators because they are not well known. People must be trained to use them. Skilled proponents are not walking the streets. Data processing managers think that application generators take as long to learn as COBOL. They are reluctant to expend the training time necessary to develop the skill in-house. However, it does not take years to become skilled in an application generator as it does COBOL. "Yes," the data processing manager will say, "application generators are great, but I can get a COBOL programmer started on the project today. I don't have the time to train them to use an application generator." And so the manager will start a COBOL programmer on a project that will take a year to program rather than spend three weeks training one to use an application generator so the task could be completed in a month.

The DP manager will also be skittish about application generators because they do not feel confident of supporting them if the vendor should disappear. "If I get stuck with a personnel/payroll system written in COBOL, I can stick any journeyman programmer on the job. If the vendor bellies up and I get stuck maintaining the generator myself, I've got to hire another intractable systems programmer to do the job." Application generators are esoteric and highly sophisticated systems.

Even though application generators are extremely powerful, they still take more effort to implement than a package. (However, it will be much faster than programming.) With a package, many of the system characteristics are predefined and hard-coded into the system. With an application generator, all this information must be specified, down to the format of the input transactions and the screens for on-line systems.

One vendor has tried to remedy this problem by providing the generator with a canned set of parameters that define a system, much like a COBOL package application. This is a good concept because having a skeleton set of parameters with which to work eliminates much of the effort. However, data processing people see the parameters as defining yet another package that does not quite fit, without seeing how easy it is to make modifications. "Oh, well, if I've got to change a parameter, I might as well program the thing in COBOL."

The authors are convinced that application generators are the next wave in software development. We believe that they represent the most significant improvement in system development productivity since the advent of on-line program development systems.

Chapter 23
Selecting Packages
for Personal Computers

Now that personal computers are being advertised on national television, now that they fill pages of advertising in news magazines, now that they are being taught to grade school children, now it is perhaps time to acknowledge them in data processing.

Data processing people have tended to turn their backs on personal computers, at least professionally. Personally, they may own them at home. There are several reasons for data processing's reluctance to embrace the personal computer. First, opening up computing to the laity might have a shattering effect on their priesthood. It is a humiliating experience for a data processing person to have a grade school child come home and ask a question about PASCAL and have to plead ignorance of the language.

Another reason for data processing not being enthusiastic about the personal computer in business is that they know from experience what ultimately will happen and that they will be left holding the bag. Throughout the company, end users are going to buy hundreds of offbeat personal computers, they are going to become afficionados of each computer's language, they are going to write complicated, undocumented applications programs on the computer that are critical to the operation of the department, and then they are going to leave the company for another job. Data processing will be called in to pick up the pieces, and it is work that they hate. As one data processing manager succinctly put it, "We are entering the age of computer anarchy."

The final reason that data processing has not become involved with the personal computer is beyond their control. End users see it as a way to do computing without having to get involved with the data processing department. Data processing does not mind this because they know that complicated computer applications are done only by programmers. If the clerks, accountants, or engineers get turned on to computing, do sophisticated applications, and become programmers, eventually all these people will migrate to the data processing department. In this sense, the personal computer is not a competitor; it is a missionary.

Data processing people may resent personal computers because they give end users a false impression of the difficulty of running and implementing systems on large-scale equipment. The personal computer owner who installs Visi Calc in an hour gets a distorted impression of how difficult it is to install packages on large computers. Packages on small computers have a very limited number of variables with which to deal. The personal computer owner does not need to worry about compiling programs, JCL, file allocation, conversion, handling union bargaining units, satisfying EEO requirements, or any of the other needs that are characteristic of large computer installations.

Perhaps the main difference is that the personal computer is just that—personal. It is not shared. There is just one user to please— one's self. There are no committees to organize, there is no multitude of users whose requirements must be resolved, and there are no egos to be stroked. Complexity goes up exponentially with the number of items that interact. If a system is built to be shared by two people, it is not twice but four times as difficult. With a personal computer, there is no need to share the computer with others, which makes the operating system immensely simpler. Problems are not solved for a group of people but for one person, which again is infinitely simpler.

Despite the arm-length attitude of data processing toward the personal computer, its appeal is overwhelming. The hardware for a personal computer generally costs less than the terminal of a big computer. Once a personal computer is purchased, the only remaining cost is for some software, a little electricity, and perhaps some supplies. Hidden behind the terminal of a large computer are line costs, layers of operating system, the hardware itself, systems programmers, and an entire data processing department. Using a large computer is expensive when one picks up the tab for all these items. A personal computer is available to an individual 24 hours a day. For a large computer at a data center to have the same availability requires three shifts of personnel.

The personal computer is simpler to use than a large computer. It was not designed by people whose overriding goal seems to be to keep systems programmers employed. Security is less of a problem. A person who wants security just locks the floppy disk in a safe. (People do not worry about their data being stolen; they worry about someone walking off with their computer.) Response time is better. Unlike many of the large computers that support hundreds of concurrent users, things happen when the ENTER key is pressed on a personal computer.

One of the ironies of data processing is that many of the technical problems that were so hard to conquer have become irrelevant with newer technology. Data processing spent the 1960s trying to provide timesharing to allow many people to share an expensive CPU. Now people can afford their own CPU in a personal computer. The 1970s were spent trying to provide virtual storage to share the expensive computer memory. Now memory is so inexpensive that virtual storage and paging have become the data processing equivalent of a plastic horse collar.

Because of all this, we will see more and more personal computers in business. As a consequence, you as an individual will likely be selecting packages for personal computers. Here is how it is done.

Rather than selecting a package for a personal computer, one must shop for it. No RFP is sent out to the vendors. The vendors probably cannot be contacted. Packages are bought in a plastic bag from a computer store. A person may need to shop from store to store to locate a salesperson who knows the software enough to help and can speak English rather than a dialect of data processing. People who work in computer stores are often passionately interested in what they sell and can be of immense help. Unfortunately, they are about the only help a person is going to get on a software package for a personal computer. It is not at all like the support there is on a large computer.

Another source of information is computer magazines, which carry articles on software. Even better are contacts. It is easy to make contacts. People who own personal computers have a common interest and love to share their experience. These people tend to spend a lot of time in computer stores. There is one special group of customers who usually loiter in the store. They look like systems programmers. They also sound like them, but they are likely to be more helpful.

Perhaps the best way to evaluate a package for a personal computer is to test the package. Some computer stores will let customers test software packages. They allow people to run the package in the store on one of their computers so that they can get the feel of using the package. They may also allow customers to look over the documentation. Usually, a copy of the documentation cannot be obtained without buying the package.

Packages for personal computers are very different from packages for large computers. They have an entirely different set of constraints. A payroll package for a personal computer usually has a limit on the number of people who can be paid and is limited to a particular state.

There are usually other software limits, such as the number of records that can be stored or processed. The packages serve a specific, limited function.

The packages also have hardware limits. They may need a particular type of disk drive, printer, or display terminal. Packages for personal computers are usually not general purpose.

The software arrives on a floppy disk. It will usually not include the source language statements. This is about the only way software vendors have of protecting their products on personal computers. And even then, personal computer owners, who may in all other respects be entirely honest, copy proprietary software on diskettes with a rapaciousness not seen since days of Attila the Hun.

Not getting a copy of the source statements for a software package means that there is no way to make modifications. If the package is not satisfactory, another one must be bought.

The selection of packages for personal computers is not as critical as it is for large computers. First, a typical package for a personal computer might cost $150 rather than the $50,000 typical for a large computer package. Blowing $150 on a package is probably not critical.

Second, the packages serve smaller, more discrete applications. A package really can be implemented on a personal computer in a few hours or days. Third, packages for personal computers are not critical to the operation of companies in the same way that an accounts payable or general ledger system is. Because the applications are smaller and less important, there is not the conversion problem that there is for big computers. The hardware, the package, and the application are all likely to be obsolete in a couple of years.

What this points out is the vast diseconomy of scale in large-computer applications. The problems of volume, of complexity, and of sharing data, which are typical of large-computer applications, increase exponentially. This is why large applications on large computers are totally unlike small applications on small computers.

In summary, personal computers, while very powerful, are generally for smaller problems. As they increase in power and begin to handle large applications, they will begin to take on the characteristics of large computers: they will be programmed by professional programmers (even if they call themselves accountants, clerks, or engineers), they will require a support staff, and there will be conversions from one computer to another.

Appendix A
List of Larger
Financial Package Vendors

American Management Systems, Inc. 1515 Wilson Boulevard. Arlington, VA 22209. (203) 841-6000

Cyborg Systems Inc. 21st Floor. 2 North Riverside Plaza. Chicago, IL 60606. (312) 454-1865

Data Design Associates. 1250 Oakmead Parkway. Sunnyvale, CA 94086. (408) 730-0100

Fortex Data Corporation. 10 South Riverside Plaza, Suite 1560. Chicago, IL 60606. (312) 454-1650

Genesys Software Systems, Inc. 10 Grafton Street. Lawrence, MA 01843. (617) 685-5400

Information Science, Inc. 95 Chestnut Ridge Road. Montvale, NY 07645. (201) 391-1600

Management Science America, Inc. 3445 Peachtree Road, N.E. Atlanta, GA 30326. (404) 262-2376

McCormack & Dodge Corp. 560 Hillside Avenue. Needham Heights, MA 02194. (617) 449-4012

Software International. Elm Square. Andover, MA 01810. (617) 475-5040

Tres Systems, Inc. 4255 LBJ Freeway. Dallas, TX 75234. (214) 233-4341

University Computing Company. UCC Tower/Exchange Park. Dallas, TX 75235. (214) 353-7334

Walker Interactive Products. 100 Mission Street. San Francisco, CA 94105. (415) 495-8811

Wang Laboratories, Inc. One Industrial Avenue. Lowell, MA 01851. (617) 459-5000

Appendix B
Information Sources
for Packages

American Bar Association. 1155 East 60 Street. Chicago, IL 60637. Publishes a report on law applications and software

Auerback Publishers, Inc. 6560 North Park Drive. Pennsauken, NJ 08109. Publishes software reports

Computer Decisions. 50 Essex Street. Rochelle Park, NJ 07662. Monthly magazine with many articles on packages

COMPUTERWORLD. P. O. Box 880. 375 Cochituate Road. Framingham, MA 01701. Weekly newspaper with many articles on packages

Data Sources. P. O. Box 5845. Cherry Hill, NJ 08034. Publishes a directory of the computer industry

DATAMATION Technical Publishing Co. 666 Fifth Avenue. New York, NY 10103. Monthly magazine with many articles on packages

DATAPRO Research Corporation. 1805 Underwood Boulevard. Delran, NY 08075. Publishes directory of applications software and ratings of software

International Computer Programs, Inc. (ICP). 900 Keystone Crossing. Indianapolis, IN 46400. Publishes quarterly software directory and six directories for specific industries

International Directory of Software. First Federal Building, Suite 401. Pottstown, PA 19464. Publishes list of 4000 proprietary software products

Kinderbilt Publications. P. O. Box 346. Plymouth, MA 02360. Publishes monthly software review

Manufacturing Software Systems, Inc. P. O. Box 278. Williston, VT 05495. Publishes in-depth evaluation of manufacturing packages

MIS Week. Fairchild Publications. 7 East 12th Street. New York, NY 10003. Weekly magazine with many articles on packages

Professionals Unlimited. P. O. Box 39123. Washington, D.C. 20016. Publishes IBM/38 software directory

Reifer Consultants, Inc. 2733 Pacific Coast Highway, Suite 203. Torrance, CA 90505. Publishes software tools directory

Software News Technical Publishing Co. 5 Kane Industrial Drive. Hudson, MA 01749. Weekly newspaper with many articles on packages; also maintains a data base of software available

Index